What people have said about Steve Clapp and Christian Community's resources on finance, faith, and hospitality

"Christian Community's stewardship resources offer a very practical approach which should produce excellent results for congregations which are facing stewardship challenges realistically."

Loren Mead
Founder of The Alban Institute

"These are great stewardship materials for local congregations."

Joanne Thomson
Associate Conference Minister, Wisconsin Conference, UCC

"*Cell Phones, Dessert, and Faith* really helped our people relate their personal finances to their spiritual lives. It increased giving in our church; but more importantly, it helped people in their lives."

United Methodist Pastor

"Using this resource increased our giving by 25 percent over the previous year." [About *The Dessert First Complete Financial Commitment Program*]

Presbyterian Pastor

"Christian Community provides a wealth of resources that should be made available to local churches."

Ivan George
American Baptist Churches

"Each resource is timely, well-written, and is based on solid theological, ministry, and educational principles."

San Francisco Theological Seminary Professor

"Bernhard and Clapp provide practical ideas that can increase the quality of hospitality.... This book has great value for pastors and the entire church." [About *Widening the Welcome of Your Church*]

Herb Miller in *Net Results*

"Our church has never been comfortable talking about evangelism, but the hospitality approach fits us very well. Studying this book has helped us learn how to do outreach in a way that fits our congregational culture." [About *Deep and Wide*]

United Church of Christ Minister

"This valuable new release deals directly with the tough questions raised by the tragic events of September 11, 2001... recognizing the presence of Christ in others can have a liberating impact on all we do." [About *Hospitality: Life in a Time of Fear*]

Church Educator

"This book will help you find meaning and purpose in a fearful world and equip people to extend healing and hope to others living in fear." [About *Hospitality: Life in a Time of Fear*]

Sheila Hoover in *Leadership Development*

"How can the church function in an environment of fragmentation, violence, and fear? These books on hospitality and faith take a practical approach, offering many excellent suggestions to congregations grappling to show hospitality in our complex time."

Mennonite Weekly

Ten Money Myths:

A Guide to Personal Finance For Christians

Steve Clapp

A LifeQuest Publication

Ten Money Myths: A Guide to Personal Finance for Christians
Steve Clapp

For further information, contact: LifeQuest, 6404 S. Calhoun Street, Fort Wayne, Indiana 46807; DadofTia@aol.com; (260) 744–5010.

ISBN-10: 1-893270-54-8
ISBN-13: 978-1-893270-54-1

Library of Congress Control Number 2009942796

Manufactured in the United States of America

Contents

This book is dedicated to my friends and colleagues in Christian Community, New Life Ministries, the Network for Charitable Giving, the Religious Institute, Many Voices, and Lincolnshire Church. It is an honor and a privilege to work with you.

My special thanks to Kristen Leverton Helbert, Stacey Sellers, and Holly Sprunger for their help with this book and to all the clergy and congregations who have cooperated with Christian Community on research and pilot projects. We are thankful for the work of our friends at Evangel Press and for their high standards in book production.

God saw everything that he had made, and indeed, it was very good.

Genesis 1:31

And God is able to provide you with every blessing in abundance, so that by always having enough of everything, you may share abundantly in every good work.

2 Corinthians 9:8

If you have come to this book hoping for counsel that will make you wealthy, you have come to the wrong source. I certainly hope that this book will improve the quality of your financial life, and I am convinced that identifying some of the harmful myths of our time can have material benefits. But my primary purpose in writing this book is to give you tools that will help you relate your financial life to your spiritual life. I am more concerned about your relationship with God and with other people than about your wealth. You will likely achieve financial benefits from reading these pages, but the achievement of those benefits is not my primary purpose.

I am not a certified public accountant or a certified financial planner, and no advice in this book is a substitute for advice from those professionals. But be sure that you choose professionals who really do have your best interests at heart. See **Myth Five** *for more cautions about even the best-intentioned professionals.*

Introduction
Myths about Money

I've had the privilege of conducting workshops on stewardship all over the United States. In 2008 I had three experiences at a Saturday workshop that I've never had before and do not expect to have again.

First, I almost lost my voice! I had a sinus and respiratory infection that affected my vocal cords. I could hardly believe it. I've had my share of allergy trouble, colds, flu, and sinus infections in the past, but my voice has never been affected. There may be people who have prayed for me to lose my voice, especially family members, but it has never happened! This time it almost did. I barely made it through the workshop.

Second, I heard a 33-year-old woman share the most candid statement about personal finances that I've ever heard made to a large gathering. There were a hundred people at the workshop; and when we were dealing with the impact of economic problems on the lives of people, she told the whole group about her situation. She told us that she and her husband were about to lose their home because of an adjustable rate mortgage. She said that they had purchased the house confident that the value would increase fast enough that they could refinance on more favorable terms before their interest rate skyrocketed. But that didn't happen.

Then she made a strong statement of faith, and I'll endeavor to use her words: "I prayed and prayed for there to be some way that we wouldn't lose our home. But we now know that it's inevitable that we will. At first I felt let down by God. Then I thought about it more and realized that God was responding to my prayers. It wasn't possible for God to increase our income or make the bank more reasonable, but it was possible for God to help us deal with our situation. We'll lose the home; but we still have a good income and can afford to rent a home that will be nice. With so many people homeless and living in unsafe conditions, we still have a great deal for which to be thankful. And someday we'll buy another home and be more careful about our commitment." Everyone present was moved by her statement of faith.

I occasionally hear people say that clergy and churches shouldn't talk much about money. Now certainly it's true that it's possible for a church to push too hard for congregational giving. But economic matters are in fact spiritual matters. They have tremendous impact on our lives. Christian Community, the organization I direct, discovered in a recent study that 91% of highly committed Christians experience strong anxiety about money at least some of the time; and 64% say that they experience strong anxiety about money almost all the time. Those percentages are somewhat higher than we found in a similar study a decade ago, but even in better economic times, money still is a frequent source of anxiety to most people, including Christians.

How we handle wealth and property are spiritual issues, and the Gospels talk frequently about these topics:

- 109 times in Matthew
- 57 times in Mark
- 94 times in Luke
- 88 times in John

Clergy and theologians often use the word "stewardship" to describe our use of the material gifts God has given us, but that isn't a word with which many of us are familiar in our culture. The Greek word for steward is **oikonomos**, which is derived from another Greek word, **oikos**, literally meaning "residence." The Greek **oikoumene** referred to the whole world or the inhabited earth. Everyone in a residence has a responsibility for the others who live there. A steward is a manager, custodian, or trustee for something owned by someone else.

Most of us aren't accustomed to thinking of ourselves as anything other than the owners of what we possess. In reality, we are all stewards of wealth and property, because these resources in fact belong to God.

Like many people reading these words, I work hard. Between my "day job" as president of Christian Community and my volunteer work for my local church, I always work sixty hours a week and sometimes much more. It's natural for us to think that we've "earned" everything that we have. But the opportunities I have are primarily because I was born into a middle-class home with parents who took education seriously and helped me earn an undergraduate and two graduate degrees. If I had been born in India or South Africa or a low-income home in the United States, my options could have been very different. The reality is that all we have comes from God; and we are custodians, managers, or stewards of it.

There's more to the story of the young woman who spoke so candidly about losing her home. A third thing happened at the workshop that I've never seen happen before. At a coffee break, an elderly farmer who was there approached the young woman who had been so candid. He didn't know her well, but he knew her parents. He told her that he had recently sold half of his farm and had the money in a low-paying certificate of deposit at his bank. He told her that he would loan her the money to get out of the adjustable rate mortgage and keep her home and that she could get a traditional mortgage sometime in the future.

She didn't share her witness thinking that someone there would solve her problem. She in fact was at peace with moving from their home to a rental property. But God is continually at work in all of our lives, seeking to bless us in ways that may be surprising. In the midst of deepest anxiety, we should always remember that God is with us and will provide. The Bible offers some important core concepts about out faith and money:

First, God will see that our needs are met. Even in times of high financial anxiety, we need to remember that God is with us. "'Therefore I tell you, do not worry about your life, what you will eat or what you will drink, or about what you will wear. Is not life more than food, and the body more than clothing?'" [Matthew 6:25] God will see that our basic needs are met, and God in fact intends to bless us with much more than we need.

Second, God wants us to share out of thanksgiving for what we have and does promise that we will have enough to do that. "The point is this: the one who sows sparingly will also reap sparingly, and the one who sows bountifully will also reap bountifully. Each of you must give as you have made up your mind, not reluctantly or under compulsion, for God loves a cheerful giver. And God is able to provide you with every blessing in abundance, so that by always having enough of everything, you may share abundantly in every good work" [2 Corinthians 9:6–8]. If we give under pressure or resentfully, we derive little spiritual benefit from that giving. When we give from thankful hearts for the blessings we have and for the good our giving can do, we ourselves are blessed in the process.

Third, God asks that we make our offerings **first** rather than out of our leftovers and that we give proportionately to what we have received. The concept of "first fruits" runs through the Old Testament. When we give with that kind of generosity, the needs of the church and society are met. In fact there would be more than enough to meet those needs if we were all that generous. The Book of Exodus talks about the overwhelming generosity of people in bringing gifts for the temple: "The people are bringing much more than enough for doing the work that the LORD has commanded us to do" [Exodus 36:5].

While this book speaks some to the matter of our financial giving to the church, the purpose of the book isn't to motivate you to be more generous in your support of your congregation and other charitable causes. The purpose of the book is to help you more firmly connect your financial resources (or lack of resources at some point in life) with your spiritual life. Financial decisions are, at the core, really spiritual decisions.

Our society and so-called financial experts have perpetuated several myths about money. The young woman at the workshop who was about to lose her home had been a victim of some of those myths, and almost all of us have been harmed by the way our consumer society teaches us to view money.

Some of these myths reflect unhealthy theology, and some reflect unhealthy financial practices. Some of these myths, when plainly stated, are clearly erroneous, like:

Your worth and happiness are determined by what you earn and by what you own.

But the fact that the myth is clearly erroneous doesn't keep us from being strongly affected by it when it is so pervasive in our society. There are some other myths that aren't as clearly erroneous, like:

Estate planning is primarily for wealthy people.

That myth is one that keeps many people from doing the planning and making the relatively inexpensive legal arrangements that would make a tremendous difference for their loved ones.

This book deals with those myths and eight others. I'll help you examine each of the myths within a Christian context and will offer some practical strategies to help you with financial decision-making.

Myth Number One

Your worth and happiness are determined by what you earn and by what you own.

This is a very pervasive myth in our culture of consumerism. And in a downward economy, this is an especially harmful myth. People who internalize this commonly held view are likely to find their self-esteem in the basement and their happiness at the mercy of forces they can't control. A deep faith and healthy understanding of Scripture can give us the perspective to find meaning and happiness no matter what the shape of the economy is.

The myth is obviously erroneous when stated this blatantly: *Your worth and happiness are determined by what you earn and by what you own.* We know that one's worth should not be determined by possessions or income, but we live in a society that acts as though this is true, and it's very difficult to escape the influence of this myth on our lives. Think with me for a few minutes about how you would respond to these questions:

- How often have you found yourself feeling secretly envious of someone who has considerably more wealth that you have?

- How often have you felt that you should have made better financial decisions and provided a more secure base for yourself and those you love? Have those feelings gone sufficiently deep for you to actually feel like a failure?

- How often have you thought you would have greater happiness if you had a larger house or condominium, a more expensive car, or the opportunity to travel more extensively?

- How often have you found yourself, though envious, also looking up to people with great financial resources? Do you feel that people like Bill Gates and Warren Buffet, for example, really are better than others?

- Do you feel at times as though persons of wealth have considerably greater influence on the events of life than more ordinary people? Do you compare yourself negatively to such persons? Or do you fear that your spouse, children, or parents compare you negatively to such persons?

- Do you have possessions that exert an unnatural or an unhealthy control over your life? Is having a particular house, car, computer, item of jewelry, work of art, or some other material possession more important to you than it should be?

If you never struggle over questions like those just raised, then you are unusual. Christian Community's research on money and the spiritual life makes it clear that most of us struggle with the connection between what we own and our worth as children of God. We may know rationally that our possessions should not determine our worth, but it's very difficult to live in this society without emotionally connecting what we have to what we are worth.

When I went through the security screening at Logan Airport in Boston on a recent trip, a young woman who obviously did not fly very often was in line in front of me. As many reading these words know, if you have a computer in your suitcase or briefcase, the Transportation Security Administration (TSA) expects you to take it out of the case and put it in a separate tray for inspection. This young woman did not know that, and there was so much confusion with the crowd of people going through the screening process that she didn't hear or understand the announcements about it. Unfortunately for her, she left her computer in her briefcase. The TSA staff person who was screening carry-ons with an x-ray machine immediately spotted the computer still in the briefcase and was furious. She yelled at the young woman, telling her that everyone knew you had to take your computer out and asking whether she thought that she was somehow too good to follow the rules.

The young woman kept trying to explain that this was only the third time she had flown and the first time that she had a computer with her. Her protests and the long line waiting to go through the screening had no impact whatsoever on the TSA employee who was determined to humiliate her. And she succeeded—the young woman broke into tears as she had to come back, take her computer out, and go through the screening process all over again.

When she took her computer out of her bag, I noticed that it was an Apple—not just an Apple in fact but the same kind that I have. Then, just as I started sending my own items through the x-ray machine, I had some bad luck of my own. I got pulled aside by another TSA employee to stand in a booth that blows air on you and presumably checks for explosive residue (or bad breath or deodorant failure or something). I had to stand in the booth like a little boy in a corner until I got the "all clear" beep.

When I came out, I went on through the conventional screening and set about collecting my belongings that had gone through the x-ray machine while I was in the isolation booth. I thought it odd that my computer was in the front tray since I always put it in the last tray so that it has the shortest time to sit there before I can join it again. I don't like to be separated from my computer! Then I looked at the bottom of the computer, and a knot formed in my stomach. I have a business card taped to the bottom, but there was no card on this computer. The very distraught young woman had taken my computer instead of hers, and it was a huge waiting area with multiple gates to the planes. I grabbed her computer and my other belongings, choosing to carry my shoes rather than take the time to put them on, and started running.

Our material possessions do become very important to us. Although I do frequent backups, the thought of losing my computer was overwhelming both because of the financial investment it represents and even more importantly because of the information on it. While I could eventually restore my programs and files, it would be a great deal of work. Our computers, our cell phones, our automobiles, our houses, our clothing, our television sets, and the rest of our possessions are important to us.

I did find the young woman at Logan Airport waiting in a gate area. I went up to her and said, "I think you have my computer." She looked at me and broke into tears again saying, "I didn't mean to steal your computer. I didn't mean to steal your computer." I reassured her that I knew she hadn't taken it intentionally; after all, she had left her own behind!

Then she started explaining to me that this was just one more in a long series of events that had been going wrong in her life. She was a university student on her way home to talk with her parents. She had been informed that week that she was losing her scholarship, which paid for her tuition and fees at the very expensive, prestigious institution of higher education she attended. She had lost the scholarship because she had let her grades slide just a little. She had felt that the nice people in the university financial assistance office wouldn't be quite as literal about the required grade average as they had turned out to be.

She told me that she had tried to find a way to borrow the money that was needed so she wouldn't have to tell her parents, but it wasn't possible for her to do that. She said that the main reason she didn't want to tell them wasn't because she felt like a failure but because the problem would make them feel like failures. Neither of her parents had graduated from college, and they had been elated when she was accepted at such an excellent university. Neither of them had high-paying jobs, and they both felt that they had made serious mistakes in their lives and were not as smart as people who were doing better financially. They would want desperately to be able to make up the difference from the loss of her scholarship, but it would be too much money. They could already barely meet the expenses that were not covered by the scholarship or by her part-time job. She knew deep in her heart that, instead of being disappointed in her for not having maintained the grade average, they would instead be disappointed in themselves for not having made more of their lives.

And then she cried as she told me how much she loved her parents, how much she admired her parents, how aware she was that they had made decisions all through her life with the major goal of helping her have a better life than they had. It broke her heart to think that her unsatisfactory study would cause them to feel negatively about themselves.

She also talked about how uncomfortable it was to be an essentially poor person on a campus that had so many people who were from affluent families. Other people thought nothing about spending money going out for lunch or supper whenever they felt like it. Her girlfriends talked continually about the clothes that they purchased. Others made plans to spend the summer in Europe or Hawaii while she made plans to go home and get as many hours of work as she could at the restaurant she had worked at while in high school. She also lamented that her friends were oblivious to the impact of their conversations and decisions on people who didn't have as much as they did. Then she said, "But they really aren't my friends. I just want them to be my friends. I envy them, and I resent them at the same time."

God really does seek to bless our lives. As I listened to her, it became very clear to me how richly she had been blessed with her parents and how richly they had been blessed having her as a daughter. Her concern was not about herself but about how what had happened to her would impact them, and they would be concerned not about themselves but about her. And all three of them stand as victims of a society that tries to convince us that our worth and our happiness are tied up in our wealth and property.

The Scriptures give a very different view of life. And while the Scriptures do not promise that we will be wealthy, they do promise that God will bless our lives. In fact the Scriptures tell us that God wants to bless us even beyond what we can ask or imagine. Consider these words from Ephesians 3:18–21:

> *I pray that you may have the power to comprehend, with all the saints, what is the breadth and length and height and depth, and to know the love of Christ that surpasses knowledge, so that you may be filled with all the fullness of God.*
>
> *Now to him who by the power at work within us is able to accomplish abundantly far more than all we can ask or imagine, to him be glory in the church and in Christ Jesus to all generations, forever and ever. Amen.*

Life in fact is filled with surprises. Sometimes we find ourselves broken-hearted over things that have been said or done to us by those we love. Sometimes we find ourselves learning and gaining from experiences with persons we do not particularly like. In Ephesians, we find Paul praying for the strengthening of the faith of his readers and reminding them of how much God is able to do in their lives—not only more than they ask for but even more than they can imagine! The young woman with the computer, the incredibly rude TSA employee, and I are all connected together—and we are all loved by God, even when we may stray far from the image in which we were created.

Many of us go through life disappointed that we do not receive some of the blessings for which we had hoped and prayed. Sometimes we wonder why God permits so many horrible things to happen. Sometimes we pray repeatedly for a relationship to be healed or for life to be made easier or for our financial health to improve and nothing seems to happen.

God does indeed overwhelm us with blessings, but not always in the ways we expect. And if we are not careful, we will go through life failing to recognize many of the blessings that we receive. I want to offer a few suggestions of ways to get more deeply in touch with the blessings God gives us and to make us more receptive to those blessings.

First, believe with the author of Ephesians that God really does desire to bless you. God desires to bless you far beyond what you can ask or imagine. And those blessings come every day. When I reflected later in prayer about the TSA incident at Logan Airport, I became aware of what a blessing it was to be able to travel by airplane to and from Boston, what a miracle that so many tons of steel can get up in the air and fly and that I could make such a trip so quickly. I became aware of what a blessing it had been to visit with my cousin Susan in Boston and to have a very productive meeting with a foundation in Boston that has funded some of the work of the organization I direct, Christian Community. I became aware of what a blessing it was to have a computer in the first place, to be able to do all that this remarkable technology makes possible. I became aware of what a blessing it was that my health is good and that I could grab my things and take off running after the young woman. How easy it is to let the frustrations of life keep us from recognizing the blessings. There is an old children's song that says, "Count your blessings, Name them one by one, Then you will see what the Lord has done."

Second, recognize that God sometimes responds to our prayers in ways we do not expect. We have an unhealthy tendency not only to present our difficulties to God in prayer but also to tell God how things should be resolved. Sometimes we will pray and pray for a relationship to be healed, and no matter how hard we pray or how hard we try, the relationship does not heal. But God's ability to help is sometimes limited by the ability of the other person to be influenced or by other factors of which we are completely unaware. Perhaps what God is really trying to give us is a sense of peace that we have done what we could and that the relationship can't become what we would like it to be. We may fail to receive the gift of peace that God is seeking to give because we continue to insist on a healing of the relationship that is not possible.

The examples are numerous. Rather than giving us the greater financial success for which we pray, God may be striving to help us better manage and use what we have already been given. But we fail to open ourselves to the guidance in our decision-making because we have determined that having more is what we need. Yet having more might in fact be spiritually disastrous for us.

And most of us have hoped and prayed for the healing of someone we loved, someone for whom we cared deeply, only to find that the healing did not happen and that the person died. But the death rate stands at 100%. These wonderful bodies were not made to last us forever. When the healing is not possible for reasons we may not understand, what God is in fact blessing us with instead is the gift of eternal life for the one who dies and the gift of a deeper love and appreciation of that person and of our own lives for those of us who are still in this life.

Third, we need to remember that prayer is not like a vending machine. This seems obvious, but the reminder is important. You know how a vending machine is supposed to work: you put in your money, you press the button representing your choice, and you get the product.

That is most certainly not how prayer works. We don't ask for something and immediately receive what we've requested. If that were the case, everyone would believe in God, and people would be doing little else except praying. But in fact we can pray for things that aren't even good for ourselves or for others. We can pray for things that aren't part of God's overall will. We can also pray for God to solve problems for us when what we need, with a little guidance from God, is to solve the problems for ourselves—this may be part of the reason that the answers to our prayers so often seem to come through another person or through something that God causes to change within us.

If you want to think of prayer as a vending machine, think of it more like the soda machine in the youth room at the church in which my office is located. For three months last year, I kept getting unexpected results when I pushed buttons on that vending machine! I most often received a Mountain Dew instead of a Diet Pepsi, though I also received Diet Pepsi instead of Cherry Pepsi and Mountain Dew instead of regular Pepsi. I'm not sure what the explanation was. Sometimes I think the vending machine people simply had a sense of humor. Sometimes I think that they ran out of what they needed to fill all the slots and just put in whatever they had with them. And sometimes I wonder if they paid any attention to what they were doing. But that may be a little closer to asking for things in prayer.... God will respond, but God may not respond in the way that we expect!

Fourth, we need to seek to be blessings to others, to recognize that God is continually striving to work through us to bring blessings to other people. What does that mean practically speaking? Here are two examples:

- It means that we recognize all of our money and material blessings as gifts from God and that we seek to be generous in our giving to the church, to people in need, and to other charitable causes. The reason that our giving to the church is so important is not primarily because the church needs the money, though of course it does, but rather because we need to give because it strengthens our relationship with Christ and reminds us that all we have belongs to God.

- It means we recognize that every person on the planet was created in the love of God. For me, it means facing the reality that TSA employees are the children of God. And that was made especially clear to me not at Logan Airport in Boston but at LaGuardia Airport in New York when a TSA employee actually apologized to me for a long wait and said, "Some days I just hate this job. Maybe most days." And I thought about what it would mean to every day do something you disliked, while I have the privilege of doing work that I like with wonderful people all the time.

And be sure of it, God is be seeking to bless you and me beyond what we ask for or even what we imagine. The blessings may come with great joy or in the midst of great adversity, but the blessings will be there. Will you and I see them? Or will we accept the mythology of a society that says our worth is grounded not in Jesus Christ but in our possessions?

Myth Number Two

God wants you to be wealthy; if you aren't, you are failing to follow God's guidance.

This myth is so closely related to the first myth that I considered combining them. The distinction, however, is an important one. The first myth says that our worth and happiness are determined by our wealth. The second myth goes a step further and says that a failure to achieve material success actually reflects a failure in our relationship with God.

Many television evangelists and some best-selling Christian authors try to convince us that all who follow God are going to be wealthy. The message is sometimes conveyed in more subtle ways—that if our lives have the right purpose and our faith is deep enough, we'll be successful not just by the standards of God but also by the standards of society. And sometimes the message is not subtle at all—we're sometimes told that generous giving to a particular ministry and following the teachings of that ministry will create wealth for us.

Many of these approaches leave the implication that the standards for success in our culture of consumerism are a reflection of God's standards. That's not the promise of Scripture. We are promised that we will always have enough to be generous and that God desires to bless us—but not all the blessings are material. We are not promised wealth, and some of the greatest spiritual leaders of all time chose to live very simple lifestyles. Our Lord appreciated the material world and turned water into wine for the wedding at Cana, but Jesus made no effort whatsoever to accumulate wealth for himself or for his disciples.

I visited two years ago with a man in Pennsylvania who is very involved in his church and who owns and manages a small factory. Two years before my conversation with him, he had 300 employees. Then changes in the economy had an extremely negative impact on his business, and he had to reduce his staff to 200 employees. Making the change was tremendously hard on him. Most of the people whose employment was terminated had worked for him for ten to twenty years and had become friends.

He told me that he had a period of time when he kept thinking about the large life insurance policies he had and about the fact that he was past the period when suicide would cause the policy benefits not to be paid. He started to think that both his business and his family would be better off if he did take his own life. It was his personal dark night of the soul. He had prayed repeatedly for God to help his business, but no relief had come. He wondered if he had in fact failed God in some important way and if the business problems were coming as a punishment.

Problems at work affect everyone—regardless of how high or low in the corporate structure one may be. On an evening when his spirits were especially low, a maintenance worker in his company knocked on his office door. The company no longer had custodial staff, and people rotated cleaning responsibilities. The employee at his door normally kept the assembly line in good repair but was taking a turn that evening at emptying wastebaskets and came into the owner's office for that purpose.

As he emptied the wastebasket, he said to the owner, "I don't think any of us can imagine what it's like for you to be trying to pilot this company through such hard times. My wife and I have both worked for you for twenty years, and this has always been a good place to work. You've always been a good employer. And we've been able to put our two kids through college because of these jobs. At least some of the time, I hope you're able to focus on all the difference you made in the lives of people for more than twenty years rather than just on the problems of the last couple of years." And it was exactly what the owner of the business needed to hear. The encouragement of the employee with those few words helped pull him back from the despair he felt and helped give him a different perspective on his problems.

Do not undervalue what you do. The compensation you receive does not reflect the importance to God and to other people of your work. You may not always see the full consequences of your efforts or of your interactions with those with whom you work in your vocation, in the church, or even in your home. When we are open to Christ in the midst of our work, we can experience what the Gospel of Matthew refers to as *the unforced rhythms of grace*:

> *Are you tired? Worn out? Burned out on religion? Come to me. Get away with me and you'll recover your life. I'll show you how to take a real rest. Walk with me and work with me—watch how I do it. Learn the unforced rhythms of grace. I won't lay anything heavy or ill-fitting on you. Keep company with me and you'll learn to live freely and lightly.* Matthew 11:28–30 [*The Message*]

Our work may not make us wealthy. The presence or absence of that wealth has nothing to do with the worth of what we do or with the quality of our relationships with God. How should we view our work?

First, if our work does not involve dishonesty or harm to other people, then our work is honorable and is a part of the care of the world that God has entrusted to us. I have a friend whose father has spent his entire adult life working in a factory doing work that is physically demanding. He's accepted every opportunity he had for overtime work, weekend work, and even holiday work. He had times when he considered changing to work that would be easier physically; but he could find nothing else that paid as well—and he cared about the people with whom he worked and felt he made a contribution to the high quality of the factory's products. Through that work, he put four children through college; and all of them have ended up in helping professions. He loved reading and study, and he instilled a love of that in his children. Some people would say that his children have ended up in more meaningful and fulfilling careers than he had; I would say that his children have their careers because of him.

We are all interconnected, and our work is interconnected. Our world needs people who stock the shelves in stores, who keep buildings clean, who collect the garbage, who build things, who manage things, who teach people, who heal people, who entertain us. Never diminish the importance of the work that you do.

Second, we need to avoid the twin temptations of our time—the tendency to either become addicted to our work or to see our work of no importance at all other than earning a living. Last year I somewhat reluctantly purchased a BlackBerry. Some of those reading these words have a BlackBerry, an iPhone, or a similar product. These aren't just cell phones. You can use these devices for e-mail and other Internet work. I can read and respond to e-mail in restaurants, in airports, on trains, in meetings, and in parks. I can also search the Internet for information from virtually any location in the United States or Canada. It's a tremendous convenience, but it also feeds the kind of addiction to work and busy-ness that many of us have in our 24/7 world. It isn't good when the buzzing BlackBerry takes priority over the people with whom one is visiting.

Many people in our time do become addicted to work. When that happens, devices like the BlackBerry move from being heaven-sent to demon-possessed. But it isn't the fault of the device; we invite the demons in ourselves.

The other temptation in our society today is to see our work as being of no importance beyond earning a paycheck that enables us to do what we want with the rest of our time and eventually to quit working. That makes work into something objectionable, something negative; and it keeps us from recognizing the contribution of our work to the betterment of the world in which God has placed us. Even the work of cleaning our homes and maintaining our yards is a part of order in the universe, a part of respecting what God has given us.

All of our work—all of life belongs to God. When we recognize that, the way we see our work, our service, our rest, and our play will be transformed. Our work is not a burden but a gift. When our work is done as a part of our spiritual lives rather than as something separate, we begin to understand the unforced rhythms of grace of which our Lord spoke. And then through us, our Lord may share the acts of grace that will transform others.

Third, we do not want to undervalue the importance of our work—we need to recognize that we may not always see the full consequences of the work that we do or of what we do for those with whom we work. Think with me again about the factory owner and the maintenance worker in Pennsylvania. Who has the more important role? Our society would say the factory owner, but that isn't necessarily true. As I listened to the factory owner tell me what the kind words of the maintenance worker had done for him, I realized that God had truly worked through those words to bring hope in the midst of despair.

God does not promise to make us wealthy. If we are wealthy, we should be thankful. Those of us living in Canada or the United States are almost all wealthy by the standards of people living in immense poverty in some other parts of the world. God loves all of us, and God is with all of us. While God may not make us wealthy, our work is important; and through that work, we have the opportunity to be blessings to others.

Fourth, it is appropriate for us to bring our financial needs and our financial longings to God in prayer. God is concerned about every aspect of our lives, including our financial well-being. There is nothing too trivial or too insignificant to be brought to God in prayer.

And we always can pray with hope because we know that God ultimately desires what is best for us and truly does seek to bless us. In his book *With Open Hands*, Henri J.M. Nouwen shares this perspective on prayers for concrete things:

> *When you pray with hope you may still ask for many concrete things; like nice weather or a better salary. This concreteness can even be a sign of authenticity. For if you ask only for faith, hope, love, freedom, happiness, modesty, humility, etc., without making them concrete in the nitty-gritty of daily life, you probably haven't involved God in your real life. If you pray in hope, all those concrete requests are ways of expressing your unlimited trust in God who fulfills all promises, who holds out for you nothing but good and who wants to share goodness and love with you. [Ave Maria Press, Notre Dame, 1995, p. 71]*

I do believe that God hears and responds to our prayers related to our personal finances, the finances of the organizations for which we work, and the finances of the congregations in which we are involved. We can remain firm in our hope that God desires what is truly best for us. Because God desires what is best for us and for all people, however, God may choose to bless us in different ways than we may anticipate and may not be able to solve all of our problems in the way that our prayers suggest. God's responses to our prayers can take many forms:

- God may help us better utilize the financial resources that we already have so that they stretch further and so that our anxiety decreases.

- God may sometimes bring new financial resources or opportunities into our lives. That certainly happened to the young woman in the workshop experience that I described in the Introduction to this book. While what many of us would describe as a financial miracle is not going to be a frequent response to our prayers, such things do happen.

- God may respond by giving us the faith and the strength that we need to make it through a difficult economic time. Our circumstances may not change, but our attitude toward those circumstances may change in ways that transform our lives.

- God may bring into our lives the opportunities or the people we need in order to improve our financial circumstances. God's responses to many of life's problems come through other people or through opportunities that we might previously have overlooked.

- God may indeed act to change and improve our financial circumstances, but the transformation may take place very gradually rather than in a sudden seemingly miraculous way.

- For a variety of reasons, God may not give us the specific financial blessings that we seek; but God will in fact give us many other blessings if we are sufficiently alert to recognize them when they come.

Thus there is absolutely nothing wrong with bringing any concern, financial or otherwise, to God in prayer. Prayer is the means through which we communicate with God and more fully open ourselves to the blessings that God seeks to share with us. We simply need to realize that God's response may differ substantially from our expectation. The fact that God does not make us wealthy doesn't mean that God has forsaken us or wants anything other than the best for us. We need to live with open hearts and open hands, trusting in God to provide for us and receiving the blessings that God gives.

Myth Number Three

Having additional money would solve all of your financial problems.

Many people are trapped into the magical thinking that a windfall of money or increase in income would solve all of their financial problems. In fact there are very few of us who have not entertained the fantasy that a major inheritance, the winning of the lottery, or another stroke of financial good fortune would forever transform our financial lives.

I heard an interesting conversation on the radio between a person who had won five million dollars in a lottery and a local talk show host. The person who had won the lottery said, "People just have no idea what a problem it is to have all this money. Oh, sure, I was able to pay off all my bills and buy a nice home for my family and for my parents. But now I keep having to worry about the money, about not losing it through a bad investment. And there are all these people who keep asking me for money for themselves personally or for the church or for some other charitable cause. I have friends wanting me to invest in their business ideas—some of them are probably good ideas, and some sure sound goofy, and I'm not sure I can always tell the difference, so I tell everybody no. The money ends up becoming a huge burden."

The talk show host responded, "I suppose it does represent a greater burden than most of us would imagine. But being poor and not having the money for your rent or your utility bill or the groceries or a prescription is another kind of burden. I think most of the people listening to this show would say they'd rather have the burden represented by five million dollars than the burden of being unemployed and broke."

The talk show host obviously made an important distinction in the relative burdens that having money and not having money represent in our lives. And I can think of almost no one who, given the choice, would not choose to have the burden of the five million dollars.

The person who won the lottery, however, had discovered what many other people have when good financial fortune came their way. Having money doesn't remove all the problems from a person's life. And history is filled with people who were blessed with great wealth and then lost it all.

What happens for most of us in life is that having an increase in income can help us for a time, but our desires often increase faster than our finances. Christian Community's research clearly shows that people of all income levels can experience high levels of anxiety about money. Just gaining more money doesn't automatically relieve us of financial anxiety. Some people, who were living well within their means at a lower income level, actually find themselves in greater financial difficulty when their incomes increase because they are tempted to start living beyond their means.

And the reality is that there are only a limited number of things that we can do to improve the amount of income or wealth that we have. We can't control what someone else leaves us in a will. Lotteries and other forms of gambling are guaranteed to cost us money; the probability of winning is always very low. Certainly working hard at our jobs and gaining more education may help us increase our incomes, but it takes years to benefit from those strategies.

The reality is that, for almost all of us, having a healthy financial life depends more on learning to live *within* the income we have than on finding a way to increase our income so that it is consistent with our desires.

When I was preparing to write this book about personal finance, I had a colleague of mine order for me a large number of books about personal finance and about money and the spiritual life. I read over seventy books on these topics in the process of preparing to write the book you are now holding in your hands. The vast majority of those books talk about the importance of distinguishing between our *needs* and our *desires*. You've almost certainly read articles or perhaps other books that emphasize the difference between needs and desires.

The reality for most of us living in North America is that our financial *needs* are generally met. Most of us have adequate food to eat, adequate shelter, adequate clothing, and basic medical care. If you have purchased this book, you are probably not doing without the most basic needs of life. If you are homeless, it's not very likely that you're reading these words. The world, however, is filled with people for whom those basic necessities are nonexistent and almost beyond hope. The truth is that most of our financial difficulties in North America are based on the *desires* that we have living in such an affluent, advertising-driven culture.

Making "Cheap" a Game

Several of the other books that I read suggest asking the reader to do an exercise consisting of listing all the *financial needs* in his or her life and then listing all the *financial desires* in his or her life. But if you are reading these words, you almost certainly are already aware of that distinction. And in our culture, many things that really are desires feel like they are needs.

I want to suggest to you a different kind of exercise which can be very effective in better understanding your personal finances and which can also help you gain some better control. **For a period of one month, purchase or commit to absolutely nothing that you do not absolutely have to have:**

- Buy the most inexpensive groceries that you can. Use coupons to lower the cost of your purchases. Buy store brands rather than name brands. Avoid the more expensive prepared foods that only require a few minutes in the microwave.

- Don't go out to eat.

- Don't make unnecessary trips in your automobile.

- Don't buy new appliances, furniture, books, magazines, clothing, makeup, cologne, or anything else that you don't absolutely have to have.

- Make a game out of being *cheap*! See how much money you can save!

Keep track of the amount of money you save by *not* buying what you ordinarily would buy. Unless you are very unusual, you'll be pleasantly surprised by the amount of money you save and will have a better appreciation for your financial situation.

If you have a high mortgage payment, a lot of credit card debt, and a couple of car payments, you may still find yourself in tight financial circumstances during the month-long experiment. If you truly avoid any new financial commitments or expenditures and still find it hard to make ends meet, then it is likely that you are carrying more debt than is manageable or healthy. I'll talk more in the discussion of ***Myth Six*** about the impact of debt on our lives and about what to do if the burden of your debts is pulling you into a financial grave.

For most of us, changes that reduce the amount that we spend are the most realistic way to gain better control over our finances and to lower our financial anxiety. My suggestion of a one-month experiment in spending absolutely nothing that is not necessary isn't intended to say that you should live that spartan an existence all the time. But you can learn a great deal from such an experience.

I've provided a form on the next page that you can use to keep track of the information gained in this experiment. The form lists expenditures and also savings. Keep track of everything that is spent and everything that is saved. The person who writes the checks for major expenditures like car payments, mortgage payments, and insurance bills should include those items in the record-keeping process. One page may be adequate for more than a single day depending on the number of expenditures that are made. When you keep track, literally, of every dime that is spent, you may be surprised by the number of expenditures in the course of a month.

You can make photocopies of the form for every member of the family, or you can simply have each member of the family keep track of his or her expenses and savings using a small spiral notebook (which is convenient) or using the back of pieces of paper that would otherwise be thrown away (which is a good ecological practice and another way to save money).

Person: ______________________________
Date(s): ______________________________

Amount Spent	Reason for Expenditure
$ ________	______________________________
$ ________	______________________________
$ ________	______________________________
$ ________	______________________________
$ ________	______________________________
$ ________	______________________________
$ ________	______________________________
$ ________	______________________________
$ ________	______________________________
$ ________	**Total Spent**

Amount Saved	Expenditure not made or savings created by careful choice
$ ________	______________________________
$ ________	______________________________
$ ________	______________________________
$ ________	______________________________
$ ________	______________________________
$ ________	______________________________
$ ________	______________________________
$ ________	______________________________
$ ________	______________________________
$ ________	**Total Saved**

Once you've completed the month-long experiment, you'll have a far better idea of the things you can do to save money. You'll also have regained some control over your personal finances. The next chapter will offer you some suggestions on how to continue improving your control over your finances on a continuing basis.

Saving Money

I want to offer here some practical suggestions on ways to save money. This is not intended as an exhaustive list. Those of you with access to the Internet can find many websites with ideas for stretching financial resources. My main hope is that the list that follows will motivate you to identify the strategies that are most beneficial in your own life.

1. Automobiles. Many people talk about the savings of buying a used car rather than a new car. It's certainly true that the depreciation on most automobiles makes the first two years of ownership the most expensive in terms of the value of the car. You have the potential to save money by purchasing a car that is two or more years old rather than a new car. That being said, however, remember that a used car with major mechanical problems may turn into a money pit rather than a bargain. Unless you are buying a car directly from someone you know and trust, you would be wise to have any used car evaluated by an independent mechanic.

Of course there is a sense in which any car is a money pit. Unlike some houses, automobiles do not increase in value over the time you own them—in fact, they steadily decrease in value. A few classic cars are the only exception to this. And you have to pay for routine maintenance, repairs, tires, license fees and/or taxes, and insurance.

When making an automobile purchase, think carefully about going used or new, about getting the best price possible from a dealer, about getting the best possible deal on any financing that you need, and about the likely long-term repair costs for the vehicle. *Consumer Reports* can be helpful in evaluating the quality of an automobile, whether it is new or used; but in the case of a used car, it's not a substitute for a good mechanic's evaluation of the specific car you are considering.

While some people say that it isn't wise to purchase an automobile from a friend, that's not necessarily true. A friend is more likely to offer you a fair price (something between the wholesale and retail value suggested in a blue book, which virtually all bankers have available), and a friend is also more likely to be honest with you about any potential mechanical problems with the automobile.

Leasing an automobile often makes possible a lower monthly payment, but you don't own the car at the end of the lease. I lease a car for business use, and that arrangement has overall been beneficial to me. The lease makes it very easy to determine the cost of the car for income tax purposes. I drive enough miles that I need to change cars every two or three years anyway, so always having a lease payment doesn't seem a problem. We always, however, purchase the car that my wife drives, which is our true family car. We pay cash for that car, and we keep it as long as possible—until repair bills are going to start becoming an issue or breakdowns an inconvenience.

Many of us fall into the trap of automatically renewing our automobile insurance coverage with the same company every year. The insurance companies know that, and we get slow premium creep along the way. Most people can save money by getting new insurance estimates every two or three years. Remember, however, that if you have two or three claims within a relatively short period of time, the insurance company will decide whether or not to continue your coverage in part based on how long you have been a customer. Rather than automatically changing your existing policy, let your agent or insurance company know when you have a better deal available and see if the price can be matched.

Having a mechanic who is skilled and who is honest will save you a great deal of money and inconvenience. Talk with others about their experiences with a particular mechanic or agency. Find a reliable person or agency, and stay with them if at all possible.

2. Houses/Condominiums. Entire books and countless newspaper, magazine, and Internet articles have been written about getting the best deal when you sell an existing house or condominium and when you purchase a new residence. As this book goes to press, people around the United States have a new consciousness that one can no longer take for granted that the value of a house or condominium is going to increase year after year. Many people have now had the painful experience of seeing their residences decrease in value, sometimes to the point that the house or condominium is no longer worth as much as the mortgage.

This change in the economic implications of purchasing a residence has some profound implications for personal finances. For a long time financial advisors would commonly tell people to purchase as much home as they could afford since it would be likely to appreciate in value more than any other safe investment they could make. But stretching finances to purchase an expensive home no longer constitutes a safe investment.

There are neighborhoods and communities in the United States where the annual increase in the value of properties has for years exceeded any reasonable expectation. Although this is little consolation to those who have been hurt severely by the collapse of much of the real estate market, the truth is that we should not have expected that the huge annual increases in value in certain parts of the country would continue year-after-year-after-year without any correction.

The changes that have happened do not mean that a house or a condominium is a bad investment. For most of us, there are many advantages to owning our own homes, including the fact that there is pleasure (along with a few headaches) in home ownership. We have a new awareness now, however, of the importance of not stretching ourselves too far financially in the purchase of a house or condominium. We also know that adjustable rate mortgages (which start with a lower monthly payment at one interest rate and then increase the payment and the interest rate at a future time) can cause enormous financial difficulties and may result in people losing their homes.

It isn't possible for me to offer an exhaustive discussion on home purchasing here, but a few guidelines may be helpful:

- Don't buy more home that you can afford. Be sure that the monthly payments are going to be comfortable for you, including any increase that could result from an adjustable rate mortgage.

- For most home purchases (unless buying a home with which you are already familiar from people you trust), use an agent who represents you rather than an agent who represents the seller. You want a person to be looking out for your interests. See ***Myth Five*** for more about dealing with professionals of all kinds.

- Be sure to have the house inspected by a reputable, independent inspector.

- Shop carefully for the best closing costs (which can save you thousands of dollars at closing) and for the best interest rate (which can save you many thousands of dollars over the period of the loan). Be sure, however, that you are dealing with a reputable lender. There are unscrupulous mortgage brokers and lenders. Deal with a lender you know something about, and don't hesitate to check with the Better Business Bureau.

- Remember that a higher down payment and a shorter number of years for loan repayment can save you huge sums of money in interest. While the fact that mortgage interest (at least as of this writing) can be a deduction on your income tax return, it's still better to pay as little interest as possible.

- Be cautious about taking a second mortgage on your home for any purpose. Some people take a second mortgage to purchase an automobile since the mortgage interest is deductible. Bill consolidation services often encourage a second mortgage to pay off higher interest credit card debt. But remember that a second mortgage eats into your equity in the home. If you hit a personal financial disaster, you may be better off owing a finance company for your car and a credit card company than having a second mortgage payment that you can't make and risking the loss of your house.

- I mentioned earlier that there are some headaches connected with home ownership. Home repairs and improvements are the most common source of those headaches. Repairs and improvements can be very expensive and can also be a major source of grief and frustration. We had a painter who took three weeks longer than promised to paint our house and who used a somewhat different color of paint than we had selected. Almost everyone reading this book knows of similar (or much worse) accounts of botched home repairs or home improvements. If you can learn how to make some basic repairs and improvements yourself, you can save substantial sums of money and grief. When selecting a person or a company to do repairs or improvement, always check references. Remember that the lowest price is not the best deal if the work is not done in a satisfactory (and headache-free) way.

3. Insurance of all kinds. I mentioned under automobiles the importance of being sure you are getting a good rate on insurance. The same is true for insurance on your home, your health, and your life. With virtually any kind of insurance, you need to check for the best rate available. Most people find it best to buy term life insurance rather than whole life or universal life insurance. Term life insurance pays nothing unless you die, but the premiums are much lower. Whole life or universal life insurance builds cash value, and you receive money from the policy without the necessity of dying! Whole life or universal life, however, builds cash value very slowly in the initial years, so it isn't a good investment unless you plan to keep the policy for at least fifteen years.

4. Travel and vacation expenses. Airline fares have for many years seemed to defy reason or logic from the point of view of the purchaser. For round-trip flights from my home in Fort Wayne, Indiana, to New York City over the past year, I've paid prices that ranged from a low of $225 to a high of $835 with around $400 being the most common price. The rates vary with the days of the week on which I'm traveling, with the New York area airport into which I'm flying, with how many days in advance I've been able to purchase the tickets, and with the special promotions that the airlines were or were not offering at the time of my ticket purchase. These have all been business trips, and I've purchased each ticket as much in advance as reasonably possible.

Increasing numbers of us make reservations using the Internet, often through a service like Expedia or Travelocity and sometimes directly with the airline. Those can be good strategies, and it can be beneficial to check with more than one site. These sites, however, "remember" that you have checked about a particular flight; and you should not be surprised when you find the cost of the flight has gone up from the last time you checked on it. They want to encourage you to purchase your ticket from them and to purchase it early; the price escalating pushes people to make fast decisions. That being said, shopping around for the best price still makes sense.

And if you are fortunate enough to find one who takes non-commercial customers, a good travel agent may still be the best source of good airline prices. Whenever possible, I make my flight reservations through an agent I've used for many years who has access to flight information that I cannot get myself—or cannot get myself without being willing to invest a great deal of time in the search process.

With car rentals, be sure you know in advance what the rate, taxes, and surcharges will be. A quote from one company may appear lower than that of another company but not all quotes include all the pricing elements. One of the most important steps in saving money on car rental is to check with your automobile insurance agent to be sure what coverage your own policy provides on a rental car. The extra charges for insurance on a rental car can add hundreds of dollars to the cost of a rental.

Obviously, shopping around for the best hotel or motel rates can have significant impact on the cost of travel. There are Internet services that offer to find you the best rate, and there are some that offer exceptionally low rates on hotels if you are willing to book a reservation without knowing the particular hotel into which you are going to be placed. These services can be of significant help, but it's very important to carefully read the terms before booking through them. The bookings are almost always nonrefundable, and the guarantees are very limited. You need to know the fine print of these services, because they mean every word of the fine print.

And of course much can be said for the benefits of taking less expensive vacations, closer to home. Camping can be wonderful fun if you like being outdoors and find setting up tents and outdoor cooking equipment an exciting adventure rather than a burden. Motor homes, campers, and other strategies that let you take the place to stay with you when you travel can have advantages for people who spend a lot of time on vacation. Many people, however, actually spend more money in the purchase and maintenance of a motor home than they would if they stayed in hotels and motels all the time. Be sure you realistically assess the costs involved with such a vehicle.

5. Appliances, furniture, and other major purchases. Most of us know that we need to be careful when purchasing appliances, new furniture, or other major items. We sometimes are trapped because an appliance, like an oven, a refrigerator, or a washing machine, breaks down and costs more to repair than the appliance is worth, putting us in the position of having to make a quick purchase decision. Even in those circumstances, however, a very short amount of time spent researching prices, features, and reliability can make a great difference. I have repeatedly found the guidance in *Consumer Reports* to be of great value, and that guidance is now available both in their printed resources and online. You can see comparisons of various brands with information on reliability, features, and value for the dollar. There are often surprises there, with the most expensive appliances not always being the best in performance or in reliability. And once you have decided on the brand that you want, shopping for price can save you large sums of money.

6. Groceries. Mortgage payments, car payments, and insurance payments are generally fixed amounts that you pay on a continuing basis. Groceries, cleaning supplies, and many other household items involve at least some flexibility. When you look up tips for savings money on these expenditures, you generally find suggestions like clipping coupons and purchasing generic products rather than so-called name-brand products. That advice is good, but it's also important to recognize that grocery stores and stores like Wal-Mart and Meijer that offer groceries along with a wide range of other products are all designed to encourage you to spend more money than you intended. Here are some of the things they do to encourage you to spend more:

- Though you may often come into the store with the intention of purchasing only a few items, you'll find that you have to walk a significant distance to find them. I once heard a marketing consultant suggest to a grocery store owner that customers would be very appreciative if things like bread, milk, juice, paper towels, and toilet paper were clustered at a convenient location near the main entrance to the store. The grocery store owner laughed, saying that the last thing he wanted to do was make it quick and easy for someone to pick up a few staples. Stores are intentionally designed so that customers spend as much time as possible and walk past as many items as possible. The longer you and I stay in the store and the more items we walk past, the more we are likely to spend.

- Many manufacturers pay what are sometimes called "stocking fees" in exchange for their items being displayed on shelves at the eye level of an adult (or at the eye level of a child for some cereal and candy products). Studies show that we are more likely to purchase items we readily see, even if they are higher in price.

- You'll often find the bakery near the entrance to the store because the pleasant aroma of freshly baked breads, cookies, and other items psychologically makes us hungry and increases the probability that we will make more purchases.

- People often make the assumption that the cost per ounce or other unit of measurement is less on larger sizes of products. Surely the 60-ounce size costs less per ounce than the 20-ounce size. But that isn't necessarily true! Sometimes the larger sizes cost more per unit than the smaller sizes. Don't assume! Read the labels carefully to be sure you really are getting the best price.

- We have been conditioned to purchase foods that are heavily processed, requiring little more than a few seconds or minutes in the microwave before being ready to eat. But we pay a high price for this convenience. When you buy fresh fruits, fresh vegetables, and fresh meat, you generally end up paying less than for the heavily processed foods. And the processed foods often have levels of sodium (salt) that are far higher than we should be eating to be healthy. Read the labels on many packaged foods and note the number of ingredients that sound more like something from the chemistry lab than from the farm. With just a little more preparation time, most people can eat far better tasting meals that are better for them and less expensive to purchase than highly processed foods.

- The items displayed along the check-out aisle are like a store-within-a-store. You'll find candy, magazines, can openers, and many other items there for you to browse while waiting to pay. The percentage of people who buy something more while in that aisle is very high.

- We also need to recognize that the nonfood items that we purchase at the same time we are shopping for groceries are often the most expensive part of what goes in our shopping cart. Think about it: razor blades, light bulbs, shampoo, deodorant, shaving cream, paper towels, toilet paper, dishwasher detergent, washing machine detergent, napkins, greeting cards, mops, and so the list continues. But grocery stores are not always the most inexpensive places to purchase those items. A separate trip to a discount store may save you a significant sum of money.

- Most of us do more economical shopping for groceries when we have a carefully prepared list of what we need to purchase AND when we have a commitment not to purchase things that are not on the list! It can also be a good idea to include on the list a subcategory of "Things Needed Soon but Not Now." Put on that list items, especially nonfood items, that you will need before long but don't have to have on this trip or perhaps the next trip. That lets you check prices and purchase those items at the most advantageous time.

7. Utilities. Heating, cooling, water usage, sewer charges, and telephone costs all can be significant. Here are just a few quick tips to consider:

- A home energy audit may save you a great deal of money. In some parts of North America, electric and gas utilities will provide such audits without charge. If they do not, they may be able to refer you to a professional who can offer the service.

- More and more people are abandoning the landlines in their homes and are just relying on cell phones. This may or may not be a good strategy for you, but it is worth consideration if you find yourself increasingly using the cell phone rather than the landline.

- Electric and gas companies sometimes offer special discounts or permit you to lock in a particular rate. Don't jump too fast to take advantage of these offers. Sometimes gas companies, in particular, will offer these when they are actually forecasting that rates will go down rather than up. But they don't share that forecast with you! Talk with someone knowledgeable, or do research on the Internet about the direction in which prices are likely to move.

- Bundled services for cable television, Internet service, and telephone service can offer substantial savings—but the savings are only relevant if you want all the services that get bundled together. Think about what you really want before making a commitment.

8. The benefit of thrift shops. Increasing numbers of people are finding that stores run by organizations like the Salvation Army, Goodwill, and other nonprofits offer wonderful savings on clothing, furniture, books, and a wide range of household items. Some Salvation Army and Goodwill stores can be gigantic with many, many choices. Many congregations and other community nonprofits have small thrift shops that are open for more limited hours. The items sold in these stores are almost always donated, and the income received from sales goes to benevolent work.

While people living in poverty have always been customers of these stores, increasing numbers of middle-class people have become aware of the great deals available in them. I'm writing these words while spending a couple of weeks on Cape Cod, one of my favorite places on the planet. My wife and her sister have had a lot of pleasure visiting thrift shops and antique stores. In that process, they've purchased some items of clothing that were as good as new for prices of $3, $4, $5, and $10 that would have cost $25, $60, and even $100 if new.

When you patronize these stores, you save money, you help recycle items that might have been thrown away, and you help the benevolent work of the organization from which you make the purchase. Everyone wins!

One person reading this manuscript before publication pointed out that middle-class people patronizing these stores may take products that would otherwise be purchased by poor people who may have greater need for them. I'll grant that can happen, but most of these stores have an adequate flow of products to accommodate far more customers than they currently have. The purchases of middle-class people still help the underlying charitable cause being supported by the thrift shop, and those purchases also benefit the financial well-being of the purchasers.

And More...

If you truly begin to focus effort on lowering expenditures, you'll be amazed at the number of opportunities that will be open. You'll find lots of information in the newspaper (assuming your lowering of expenses doesn't cause you to stop taking the local newspaper), on the Internet, and through your friends.

Remember... you may not always be able to increase your income, but you can exercise greater control over your expenses.

Myth Number Four

You can't manage your finances without a budget, and a budget is a great deal of work.

When I was a junior high school student, my parents decided to give me some better experience in handling money by a combination of increasing my allowance AND making me responsible for a larger portion of my expenses. I continued to have certain chores or tasks for which I was responsible because I was part of the family. My allowance wasn't directly tied to those tasks, but it was expected that I would do the tasks and that I would manage my money carefully.

There were other chores that I could do, if I chose to, for which I would receive additional compensation. I could also receive pay for working in the restaurant owned by my father. The allowance, however, was intended to cover most of my expenses. And along with the allowance came a system of envelopes to help me manage it. My parents helped me develop that system which included a separate envelope for each of the following:

- The church. I was expected to give 10% of my allowance and also 10% of any money that I earned to the church.

- Clothing. I needed to accumulate money from my weekly allowance for any major expenditure like a letter jacket or new shoes. If I wanted something especially nice, I would need to earn additional money to make it possible.

- Summer vacation. I needed to save during the year for things that I would want to do or purchase when we went on family vacation and when I went to camp.

- School expenses. I was responsible for purchasing notebooks, pens, pencils, paper, and pretty much anything else needed for school.

- Recreation. This included movies, golf, meals with my friends, and pretty much anything recreational or social that I did. When I reached the age for a driver's license, this category would be expanded to included money spent on gasoline and dates.

- Savings. I was expected to put aside 10% of my allowance and also 10% of any money that I earned to save for the expenses of college and for my future. This money was deposited in a savings account at the bank once a month.

They gave me my allowance in a combination of dollar bills and change so that I could put the appropriate amount in each envelope. This was a good system for me, and I used it until my senior year of high school. During the summer before my senior year, as I was earning more money than in the past, my parents encouraged me to add a checking account to the savings account I already had and to start keeping track of my money on paper rather than in the envelopes. Because of the years using the envelope system, the transition was a relatively easy one.

That was a system of budgeting that was pretty easy for an adolescent to use, but it taught me some very important things about money:

- I learned the value of saving for future needs—not only for college but for more immediate needs like a sport coat, summer camp, or prom.

- I learned that you can't spend everything that you receive as soon as you receive it unless you want to be caught without needed money in the future.

- I learned that it was easy to give 10% to the church when you did it all the time, setting the money aside as soon as you received funds.

- I learned that what I had previously considered insignificant expenses for school supplies cost more than I had realized when my parents had simply purchased them for me.

- I learned that I needed to earn additional money for some things that I wanted to do rather than simply trying to persuade my parents to pay for my desires.

I know those early experiences were valuable to me in handling money as an undergraduate, as a graduate student, as a minister, and as a person responsible for the operation of a nonprofit organization. My graduate business courses were easier because of the early experience in handling money.

How Much Focus on Money?

Most of the popular religious and secular personal financial management programs that are sold involve complicated budgeting forms and record-keeping that look very intimidating to the average person. People who did not grow up with the kind of experience my parents gave me in handling money often feel overwhelmed by efforts to establish a budget and to maintain the records that go along with managing finances to stay within a budget.

Some people are not sure just how much energy they want to put into managing money in their lives. They observe people who seem obsessed with money and seem to view money as more important than relationships. There are others who move from one financial crisis to another and who are so depressed about money that they want to give no more time to it than absolutely necessary.

I find it helpful to think about four types of people in terms of the focus of their lives and their knowledge about personal finances:

Type One Focus: Catastrophe Financially unaware	**Type Three** Focus: Money Financially aware
Type Two Focus: Life Financially unaware	**Type Four** Focus: Life Financially aware

Type One—Living with Catastrophe: Persons who are financially unaware and who find themselves living with financial catastrophe as a result. But it actually isn't just catastrophe in finances; it becomes catastrophe with relationships and the rest of life because of the enormous stress caused by the financial problems. These are people for whom financial problems dominate all of life. While it is very true that money won't buy happiness, not having enough money and not being wise enough about how to utilize it can sure destroy happiness for most of us. None of us wants to live like that.

Type Two—Good Life under a Shadow: These are persons who appropriately have their major focus on life rather than on money. The only problem is that they are financially unaware; and as a result of that, they are living under a shadow. A financial disaster can readily push them into a Type One life.

Type Three—Money as Priority: These are persons for whom the making of money, the spending of money, and the saving of money are the real priority in life. They may talk as though and even occasionally act as though other things are more important than money, but that isn't the case. They have high financial awareness, but they are also likely to have a low quality of life.

Type Four—Life with Financial Health: This, to me, is the healthy way to live. These are persons who are focused on life rather than on money. They recognize that there are many things that are more important than money and that money is really a tool for the enhancement of life. But these are people who are very financially aware. They have learned how to make good financial decisions and have a good understanding of how money impacts their lives.

Type Four represents where most of us want to live, where most of us should live. You don't have to have a sophisticated budget to be a Type Four person or family, but you do have to have a good understanding of what your income and expenses are and of how to make good financial decisions.

This book as a whole attempts to provide you with the outlook and the knowledge that you need to understand your personal finances and to make good financial decisions. In this chapter, I want to encourage you to get a good handle on your income and expenses whether through a traditional budget or in another way.

Getting a Grip on Income and Expenses

The envelope system that my parents taught me as a junior high boy actually embodies the basics of budgeting. It was a clear system of knowing how much money I had, how much I needed for various purposes, and how to spend the money consistently with my intentions. When I used the system properly, I always had the money I needed for major purposes, for summer travel, and for the other things I wanted to do. I also gave money to the church and saved money without any particular effort or strain.

If you do the exercise in the previous chapter that involves spending as little as possible and keeping track of what you spend and what you save, then you have the foundation for better control of the income and the expenses in your life.

Obviously the envelope system that I used as a junior high and a high school student was a cash-dependent system. That same system doesn't work very well for most of us living in a society in which many of us use very little cash. Debit and credit cards have become the basic means by which most of us pay for our groceries, buy gasoline for our cars, pay for meals in restaurants, and purchase gifts in stores.

As I started managing more money, there was a transition from my cash system to a system more based on a checking account. But even that is changing with many of us paying our bills by credit card or by electronic funds transfer or electronic checks.

In terms of always knowing where I stood financially, there were some advantages to the system of cash in envelopes. I could readily tell whether or not I had the needed money to do something. There was no temptation to charge a purchase for which I might have difficulty making payment later. That's one of the reasons why consumer experts attempting to help a person in serious financial trouble often recommend cutting credit cards in two or putting them in the freezer! A move to cash steers people away from temptation and helps them have better control.

I'm not advocating that kind of move for most of us. There are enormous advantages to credit and debit cards and to electronic banking. What remains important, however, is that we need to know how our expenditures are relating to our income.

And it's impossible to know that without an accurate idea of both income and expenses. That's what a budget really is: a realistic view of the income we have available and of the expenses that we need or want to pay. The thirty-day experiment on recording both expenditures and money saved can provide you with some of the core information for developing and maintaining a budget that will work for you.

Your Income and Expenses

The pages that follow offer forms that you can utilize to estimate and later record your monthly income and expenses. You'll find estimating the expenses much easier if you actually keep track of them for a month, as suggested in the previous chapter.

My suggestion is that you make a couple of photocopies of the pages that have the categories and the blanks. The forms are also at Christian Community's website, www.churchstuff.com, so you can download the forms from there if you prefer. You can use one copy to record your estimates of monthly income and expenses. Then you can use the other copy to enter your actual totals for a month. If you find that you like this system of recording income and expenses, you can continue to utilize it. There are, however, alternatives for those who find this procedure laborious.

What you should absolutely do is estimate your monthly income and expenses; that is an important guide for getting control of your finances. The record of spending that you may keep for any given month won't always reflect the quarterly, semi-annual, or annual expenditures for which money also needs to be put aside. For those items, record the amount of money that needs to be set aside each month in order to meet the quarterly, semi-annual, or annual bill that will come.

For the most part, these categories are self-explanatory. I have offered some notes that follow the forms to answer questions that you might have.

Income Category	Monthly Income
Income Person One	$________________
Income Person Two	$________________
Interest Income	$________________
Other Income	$________________
Total Monthly Income	**$________________**

Savings Category	Savings Expense
Retirement Payment Person One	$________________
Retirement Payment Person Two	$________________
401(k) or Similar Payment	$________________
IRA or Similar Payment	$________________
Stocks/Bonds/Mutual Funds	$________________
Savings Accounts	$________________
Whole Life Insurance	$________________
College Savings Program	$________________
Other Savings	$________________
Total Monthly Savings	**$________________**

Giving Category	Monthly Expenditure
Giving to the Church	$________________
Giving to Other Charities	$________________
Giving to Family/Friends	$________________
Total Monthly Giving	**$________________**

Tax Category	**Monthly Expenditure**
Federal Taxes	$______________
Social Security/Medicare	$______________
State Taxes	$______________
Local Taxes	$______________
Property Taxes	$______________
Total Monthly Taxes	**$______________**

Home Expenses	**Monthly Expenditure**
Mortgage Payment or Rent	$______________
House Improvements/Repairs	$______________
Home Insurance	$______________
Water Utility Bill	$______________
Electricity	$______________
Gas/Oil/Heat-AC Expense	$______________
Yard Work/Maintenance	$______________
Total Monthly Home Expenses	**$______________**

Debt Expenses	**Monthly Expenditure**
Credit Card Payments (past debt)	$______________
School Loan Payments	$______________
Other Debt Payments	$______________
Total Debt Expenses	**$______________**

Transportation Expenses	**Monthly Expenditure**
Automobile Payment One	$_______________
Automobile Payment Two	$_______________
Automobile Maintenance/Repair	$_______________
Automobile Insurance	$_______________
Other Transportation Expense	$_______________
Total Monthly Transportation	**$_______________**

Food and Entertainment	**Monthly Expenditure**
Groceries/Household Items	$_______________
Restaurants	$_______________
Vacations	$_______________
Movies, Plays, Concerts	$_______________
Other Recreation/Hobbies	$_______________
Recreational Vehicles	$_______________
Christmas and Birthdays	$_______________
Total Food and Entertainment	**$_______________**

Clothing & Child-Raising	**Monthly Expenditure**
Clothing—adults	$_______________
Clothing—children	$_______________
School Expenses	$_______________
Lessons, Fees, Etc.	$_______________

Children—allowances	$__________
Total Clothing & Child	**$__________**

Health and Insurance Expenses	**Monthly Expenditure**
Medical/Dental/Eye Expenses	$__________
Prescription & Over-the-Counter	$__________
Health Insurance	$__________
Life Insurance	$__________
Disability Insurance	$__________
Other Health and Insurance	$__________
Total Health and Insurance	**$__________**

Other Categories	**Monthly Expenditure**
________________	$__________
________________	$__________
________________	$__________
Total Other Categories	**$__________**

Total All Monthly Expenses	**$__________**

Notes on Income and Expense Categories

Income Categories: Record here the monthly income that you receive. If two members of the household are employed or have pension incomes, those would constitute Income Person One and Income Person Two. Record the amount of money received before withholdings, since withholdings are covered in the expense category. You want to see in this section the total amount of income that is available every month. Only record interest income if that is income that you receive and use. Don't record interest that you are simply letting accumulate in a savings account, money market account, or certificate of deposit. The "other" category is for additional income that you may be receiving from a legal settlement or some other source.

Some persons may have more than a single source of income from working two jobs or from having multiple pensions as well as social security. For the purposes of this form, combine those into a total income for each person.

Savings Category: Many people are make payments into retirement accounts through their place of employment, generally through withholding from income. Insert those payments for Person One and Person Two in the household as relevant. Also insert money set aside, whether by withholding or another way, for a 401(k); IRA; stocks, bonds, or mutual funds; and savings accounts.

Record insurance payments here only if it for whole life insurance which accumulates cash value; if you have term life insurance, the payment should not be recorded here. If you have a college savings program for one or more children, insert that amount and then any additional money that you save for the future.

Giving Category: A tithe or 10% of income has been for centuries the most common measure for appropriate giving to the church. Myth Nine deals with the reality that there are some persons on limited incomes for whom 10% may be too much and that there are some persons who have been richly blessed who should be giving much more. You may decide after reading about that myth to come back and adjust the figure that you insert here. For the present, write in the amount that you currently give *or that expresses what you feel you should be giving.*

Also include in this category money that you give to other charitable causes that are recognized nonprofit organizations. Some people find themselves giving significant financial help to family members or friends who are going through a hard time, and that giving isn't tax deductible. You should, however, include here any money that you share in that way with family or friends.

Home Expenses: A significant portion of the income of most people goes to housing expenses. These categories are pretty self-explanatory. Most people who are purchasing a home or own a home need to be setting aside some money each month toward the cost of home improvements and repairs. Home improvements are things that you plan in advance to do to enhance your home. Repairs aren't always planned in advance: hot water heaters go out, drains have to be professionally unplugged, furnaces have to be repaired, and so the list continues.

Debt Expenses: The largest debts most people have are home mortgages, often followed closely by automobile payments. Those items are categorized under home expenses and transportation expenses rather than here. In this category, list other debts that you are repaying. Include here the portion of credit card payments that you are making against debt you already carry on one or more credit cards rather than payments made on credit cards for current expenditures.

If you have balances from the past on credit cards, you need to recognize the payments on those as debt reduction. School loans are another very common source of debt for people in their twenties, thirties, and even forties. Also record any other regular payments that you make on debts.

Transportation Expenses: Record here automobile purchase or lease payments, maintenance expenses, and insurance expenses for the car or cars in your household. There's also a line for other transportation expenses. For many people, the "other" category will be train and bus fares. A few people have expenses for an airplane, boat, or other vehicle. If the vehicle is truly used for basic transportation, then the expense should be recorded here as "other." If the primary purpose of the vehicle is recreational, then that should be recorded under Food and Entertainment. Payments for a third or fourth automobile should go in the "other" category.

Food and Entertainment: Grocery expenditures are a big item in most household budgets, especially households with children. And of course we recognize that many expenditures in grocery stores are for cleaning supplies and other nonfood items. For purposes of this form, record grocery expenditures and expenditures for similar food and nonfood items made at other places as one category.

The other categories are fairly self-explanatory. "Other Recreation/Hobbies" may include the cost of hobbies that you have such as golfing, knitting, quilting, bicycling, or running. If you have one or more recreational vehicles, then record any purchase or lease payments as well as fuel and maintenance costs. Most households spend enough on Christmas and birthdays to warrant a separate category.

Clothing and Child-Raising: For clothing expenses, note that there is one line to record the expenses for adults in the household and a separate line to record the expenses for children. The costs of clothing for children often mount up more quickly than we expect. Young children outgrow clothes quickly, and older children are often very concerned about wearing clothes that are consistent with what other people their age wear.

Use the school expense line to record all the costs related to school for everyone in the household with the exception of young adults who are paying their own college or trade school expenses. For preschool, elementary school, middle school/junior high, and high school students, this will include fees, books, supplies, and related costs. If you have preschool tuition or private school tuition, include those expenses here as well. If there are people in the household who are in college or trade school, then expenses recorded here may include transportation and lodging as well as tuition, books, and fees.

Also record allowances that are paid to children in the home. If you are not currently giving an allowance to each child (other than preschool or toddlers!), give serious consideration to doing so. As I shared earlier in this chapter, my early experiences handling an allowance helped teach me some valuable lessons about money and about life.

Health and Insurance Expenses: On the first line, record physician, hospital, dental, and eye care expenses that are not paid by your insurance company. If you receive chiropractic care, physical therapy, or care from other medical professionals, those should go on this line as well. The next line is for the prescription and over-the-counter medications that you buy. Do not include amounts that are reimbursed or paid directly by your insurance company. For some persons, especially those seventy years of age and older, the cost of medications can be a very significant part of the budget.

This is also the section in which to include insurance expenses that have not been covered in earlier categories. Do not include the cost of health insurance that is paid for by your employer, but do include any payment which you make that is deducted from your paycheck. Life insurance and disability insurance should also be recorded on the appropriate lines, but again do not include amounts paid by an employer. The "Other Health and Insurance" line is for expenses that do no fit into one of the earlier categories.

Other Categories: I've attempted to provide the categories that will be useful to most people developing a budget and tracking expenditures. Each individual and each family, however, is unique. You may have significant expenses that do not fit into any of the categories I've provided. If that's the case, then add your own categories as needed.

The Purpose of Budgeting and Tracking

When you've completed the form provided with estimates of your monthly expenditures for each category, what you've done is develop a budget. If you find that the total expenses exceed your income, then obviously you need to take some steps to get expenses lowered. The previous chapter has a number of suggestions for saving money.

I'm hoping you'll try using the format to track your expenses for at least one month after you've developed the budget. Then you can decide whether or not it is worthwhile to continue doing so. Remember that ***the purpose of budgeting and of tracking expenditures is to have a hold on your personal and family finances.*** You don't necessarily have to do a detailed tracking every month. What's important is to have the knowledge of how much income you have and of how much you need and can afford to spend each month. As long as your income is not exceeding your expenses, it isn't necessary for most people to keep detailed records by category.

Here are some of the approaches that people use on a continuing basis:

1. Develop the budget, but don't worry about monthly tracking unless there is a problem. Some people develop a careful estimate of income and expenses like the process just outlined in this book but then do not worry about detailed tracking through the year. Around the middle of the year and at the end of the year, they take another look at their estimates and make any needed changes. If they find at any time during the year that they are starting to run short of money, then they go back to their income and expense estimates to see what has changed.

2. Keep track of expenses but don't worry about putting them into categories each month. Some people don't worry about tracking by categories of expenses but do keep a running list of money spent either in a spiral notebook or on a computer spreadsheet. This is similar to the recording of expenses that was recommended in the previous chapter. This can be easier than placing the expenditures into the kinds of categories offered in this chapter but can be very helpful if keeping expenses under control is a major concern.

In an experiment with a hundred households around the country, Christian Community asked half of them to simply record expenses each month for a year, and half of them not to worry about doing it. The fifty households who simply recorded their expenses each month ALL reported that recording the expenses caused them to spend less than if they had not done so.

3. Develop the budget, and keep track of expenses by category every month. Some people want to maintain a monthly tracking system like the one shared in this chapter. They keep a running list of their expenses and then at the end of the month divide them into the categories suggested here. Another alternative is to create a separate page in a spiral notebook for each category and then to record the expenses as they are made on the appropriate page. Then it's just a matter at the end of the month of adding the expenditures recorded for each category. They find that doing this is a good investment of time and energy. This may or may not be the case for you.

4. Use computer software to help you monitor your expenses. Some people find it very helpful to use computer software to track their expenditures. If you are comfortable working on a computer and want to have a good handle on your expenses, there are several software programs that can be of help. I'll mention three of them here. I have no financial interest in any of these organizations, and there are pluses and minuses to each of the services offered. If you want to use your computer for budgeting purposes, I would recommend your checking out all three options. You may also want to talk with friends, family members, or coworkers to see if they have other recommendations to offer.

Quicken software is extremely popular both for individuals and for small businesses. It enables you to keep close track of your income and expenses, and you can even use it to prepare checks. It also has the advantage of there being so many people who use it that you probably already know someone who can offer you assistance if you have problems.

Mint offers you online budgeting software and a significant number of services at no charge. They will recommend some services to you (such as a credit card with a lower interest rate than you are currently paying). If you elect to accept their recommendation, then they receive a nominal fee from the company providing the product or service.

Wesabe offers similar budgeting tools but has worked to create a sense of online community. Persons who use Wesabe post questions and suggestions, and others in the community respond. While not all of the advice is equally good, you can receive a number of helpful tips on personal finances.

> ***Remember: It is impossible to get control of your finances unless you make a reasonable estimate of income and expenses. You may not have to do detailed tracking, but most people will spend less if they record their expenditures.***

Myth Number Five

Salespeople, financial planners, stockbrokers, and bankers have your best interests at heart.

I have a friend who, during a time of tight personal finances, decided he was no longer going to trade cars at the same frequency he had in the past. The decision was a disappointing one for him because he loved getting a new car.

Shortly after making this somewhat painful economic decision, he had his automobile in the service department of the dealership from which he'd purchased it and was browsing on the showroom floor while waiting on a few simple repairs. A salesman approached him, introduced himself, and started talking about the new cars. My friend made a point of telling the salesman early in the conversation that he was not in the market for a new car because it was a time of tight finances with medical bills and a son in college.

His not being in the market for a car did not deter the salesman who continued to show him the features of the new models and to point out the superior gas mileage. My friend, seeking to further emphasize his lack of interest in a new car, mentioned that he was putting off a couple of not immediately essential repairs on his current car because the repairs were too expensive. The salesman grabbed hold of that opening to explain how much better it would be to be making payments on a new car that gave better gas mileage than to be dealing with the lack of predictability of repairs that would be needed the longer he drove his current car.

The initial logic of that approach connected with the "I'd sure like to have a new car" desire that was already present, and my friend soon found himself sitting in the dealership credit manager's office signing the forms to trade his car that was still in the service department and to purchase a new one. It would be a few weeks later, as he kept juggling his personal finances, that he would fully realize what a bad decision he had made. He had owed no money on his other car, and he only had 42,000 miles on it. While the car did need some work, it would have served him well, without car payments, for another two to four years. The savings in improved gas mileage and lower repair costs did not begin to compensate for the payments that came due each month.

The salesperson at his dealership was not a bad person. His job, however, was to sell cars. It wasn't his job to give objective personal financial advice to the person making the purchase. My friend, whose basic nature is trusting, made the mistake of thinking that the salesperson's logic could be trusted. It couldn't.

I'm not intending here to be disrespectful of automobile salespersons. I've dealt with the same Buick salespeople, my friends John and Mike Kelley, for over fifteen years now precisely because they are always honest and always seek to do the right thing for customers.

But it isn't their job or any salesperson's job to tell you whether or not you can afford a purchase. They also can't tell you how right a decision is for you at a particular point life. The same is true for a large number of people to whom we tend to look for guidance in managing the affairs of our lives.

There are professionals who work hard to convince us that the quality of our lives can be greatly improved by the right car, the right house or condominium, the right bank, the right investment program, or the right insurance. Most of these professionals are good people, and these are professions found in most congregations.

The reality, however, is that we are in a consumer-driven culture; and these professionals only make money when their customers spend or invest money. People who want to have healthy financial lives must learn how to avoid being overly influenced by the intended and unintended pressure of others. Too many people have been talked into houses and cars they can't afford and investments that carry too much risk for their life situation.

Two years before the stock market significantly declined, I was on a panel with a stockbroker and a financial planner talking to a large gathering of church members about personal financial management and retirement. Both the stockbroker and the financial planner talked at length about the importance of having an aggressive investment strategy if you didn't want inflation to destroy the value of your savings. Both of them spoke as though it was inevitable that the stock market would always go up, that downturns were so temporary as not to be worried about.

I made what they considered a foolishly conservative observation when I said: "The main objective in a savings program or in a retirement planning program is not to lose money. Over the course of years, compound interest at a reasonable rate can bring about a very solid return. For the ordinary person, that's far more important than making investments that will bring you a high rate of return but that inevitably carry significant risk."

Both of them said that my point of view was much too conservative and that the kind of diversified investment strategies they were suggesting were absolutely safe. I wonder what those same people were saying after the very significant fall in stock market values that came before and immediately after Barack

Obama was elected president. As this book goes to press, we have seen some return in stock market value, but it will take years for many people to recover what they lost.

Of course the reality is that an appropriate investment strategy depends on one's age and life situation. Certainly there are good reasons for younger persons to invest more aggressively than persons right on top of retirement age. But the reality is that stockbrokers and financial planners do not make as much money when people place substantial amounts of their savings in long-term treasury bills, conservative mutual funds, or other instruments where they leave the money for long periods of time.

It's not that the stockbrokers and financial planners are bad people or don't care about their clients. It's rather that self-interest can blind them to what may be the best strategy for their clients. And a stockbroker or financial planner in his or her thirties or forties is not always able to fully understand the impact of risk on people in their fifties or sixties.

I think of a wonderful couple I know in their eighties who saved and invested prudently all of their lives. They've been extremely generous with their congregation and with persons in need, giving away probably 30% of their income each year for the last decade. They trusted the management of the majority of their funds to a financial planner and a stockbroker. When the stock market started falling, their planner and their broker counseled them to "sit tight because it always comes back and won't take long." The values, however, kept falling.

By the time the couple felt sufficient panic to go with their own instincts rather than those of their planner and stockbroker, their net worth, what they had worked a lifetime to create, had declined by almost 45%. That decline has not only impacted their charitable giving, it's directly impacted their lifestyle. The advice they received, the advice they trusted, was simply not good advice. Neither of them will live long enough to recover what has been lost, no matter how well the stock market does in the future.

And Then There Are the Less than Completely Honest

A few years ago, I helped a woman who was a family friend in the process of trading cars. She was single and felt that salespeople were a little too inclined to take advantage of her. The dealerships to which I would have preferred taking her didn't sell the kind of automobile she wanted!

Once we had determined the kind of car and equipment that she desired, we started going to different dealerships to compare prices. The process was fascinating. The list prices on the cars she priced ranged from $27,400 to $27,825, depending on the specific equipment on cars the dealers had in stock. That's a narrow range. But here are the four estimates on the cost of trading cars that she received (the cost of the new car minus the value of her trade-in and any additional dealer discounts, but not including taxes or license fees):

- $11,475
- $12,300
- $13,500
- $15,650

The difference from the lowest price to the highest price was $4,175! That's a great deal of money! And the highest price to trade was actually on the least expensive car ($27,400), which makes the difference even greater. The dealership that asked for the most money emphasized what a great deal it would be and said that they were giving her top dollar for her trade. Top dollar? I don't think so.

There are some people who feel that the goal of the dealership in such transactions should be to make as much money as possible. If buyers aren't sophisticated enough to compare prices or to have done their homework, then they shouldn't receive as good a deal. It may be legal, but that doesn't make it right. Car dealers need to make a profit, and I have no argument with that. But it feels to me just plain wrong to tell someone they are being offered top dollar for a trade-in and a great deal on a car when the price is actually four thousand dollars higher than another dealer who still anticipates making money on the transaction.

I have a friend who was told by the service department at a dealership that he needed a long list of repairs to keep his car in good condition. The recommended repairs totaled $2,485. I recommended checking with an independent mechanic I knew who looked at the automobile and recommended repairs totaling $675. That's quite a difference! That much money constitutes more than a difference of opinion; it reflects the service department wanting to do unnecessary work.

Car dealers and car maintenance are easy targets for criticism. These aren't the only places one can end up getting soaked with inflated prices or unnecessary work. . . .

A few years ago our dentist retired and sold his practice to another dentist. The new dentist brought many changes to the practice including the installation of televisions in each of the rooms so that one could watch infomercials while waiting on

Novocain to do its numbing. The infomercials were pretty numbing themselves, offering very expensive services.

The cost of a trip to the dentist went up rapidly, and each trip brought the admonition to have yet another procedure done. My wife and I realized that we truly did not know how important the work being recommended was. And then the obvious occurred to us: there's something fundamentally wrong with going to a professional you feel may actually be misleading you.

We talked to good friends of ours and got the recommendation for a different dentist. We made the change, and the difference was significant. We have a wonderful dentist now, and we no longer worry about whether something he recommends is necessary. We know that we can trust him.

As I shared in the first part of this chapter, most professionals are good people—they simply are focused on the sale of their services and can't be expected to be objective concerning decisions that impact your finances. There are, however, some professionals who in fact are less than honest and sell unneeded services.

Or in some instances their desire to succeed has simply caused them to start looking at situations in ways that serve their own goals or organizational goals without carefully considering the impact on consumers. When my mother had a heart attack, she had a routine cardiac catheterization to discover how damaged her heart was and what the blockages were like. The cardiac surgeon who looked at the results felt that she should have open heart surgery.

The family physician and the internist who specialized in cardiology looked at the same results and felt that open heart surgery would be extremely hard on my mother at her age and that non-surgical treatment could bring a good result. Her own body was already forming collaterals to go around the most serious blockage, and the other blockages were not that severe.

Was the cardiac surgeon dishonest? I don't think so. But his perspective was shaped so strongly by his specialization and by the need of the hospital to utilize the expensive surgical suites that had been installed for these procedures that it was difficult for him to look at my mother's case objectively. The family physician and the internist had less baggage to influence their assessment of the situation.

Three Cautions

1. Remember that you are the one who must be in charge of your financial decisions. Don't turn that responsibility over to a banker, a stockbroker, a financial planner, a salesperson, an insurance agent, or any other professional. Be clear on your goals, and don't let yourself be talked into unwise decisions because you like the professional or want to gain his or her respect.

2. Do business whenever possible with people you know to be honest. When people treat you well and treat you honestly, respond to that by being loyal with your business. If you are dealing with people who don't feel completely honest, then start looking for another provider.

3. When making a major decision that involves your finances—and even more when it involves your health as well—it almost never hurts to get a second opinion. My mother was certainly glad that she did!

Myth Number Six

Debt is always good or always bad (depending on the "expert" involved).

I recently learned about an interesting real estate tactic. In some markets where the value of real estate declined significantly, real estate agents began a dubious process involving "short selling." The agent looks for clients owing more on a house than the current value of the house. The agent then finds the clients a new house similar to the one they already have but selling for much less money than they owe on their house.

The clients purchase the new house for the lower price than their current mortgage. Then the real estate agent suggests that they stop paying the mortgage on the old house and predicts that the bank or mortgage company will end up letting them sell the house at a loss rather than going through the process of foreclosure (this is the "short sale"). Obviously this doesn't do good things for the credit rating of the people doing the deal; but having purchased a new house, they may not be concerned about that for a few years.

This is a strategy that only works for people with good enough credit to get a new mortgage before their existing mortgage is paid off. In some instances, they may be able to get a motivated seller who can afford to self-finance the transaction.

Do you find this tactic hard to believe? If so, you can read about its use in Las Vegas in the August 24, 2009 issue of *Time*. That isn't where I first learned about it, but Las Vegas appears to be a place where the practice is becoming relatively common as this book goes to press. Of course books have a long shelf-life, so the practice may not be so common by the time you are reading these pages.

The fact that such a tactic is practiced is the result, of course, of significant loss in the value of homes. This isn't a strategy that I would recommend for two reasons. First, it just plain feels unethical. Second, the consequences to one's credit rating will hang around for several years; and it isn't safe to assume that the credit rating won't matter for awhile because one has a mortgage on the new house. Credit ratings can impact our lives in many different ways (including eligibility for certain kinds of insurance), and there is no guarantee that one might not need to relocate sooner than expected.

There are people, however, who end up unintentionally doing something very similar. They owe more money than their house is worth and then suffer a significant income loss and can't make the payments. The house ends up reverting back to the financial institution. When things improve, the people who lost the house purchase a new one for what may well be a lower price.

I've opened the chapter with the preceding real estate illustration simply to illustrate the complexities of debt in our lives. Very few people are able to make as major a purchase as a house without going into debt, and many others can't purchase an automobile without debt. Loans are the only way that some people are able to attend a technical school, college, or university.

When I read through the seventy books on personal finance and on money and the spiritual life in preparation for this book, I found two divergent schools of thought. The books by secular authorities talk about the place of debt in our lives, urging caution but also recognizing that there are times when debt is appropriate.

Most of the books by Christian authors presented an extremely negative view of debt. Some suggested that a Christian should never be in debt for anything other than the purchase of a house, and a few even maintain that you should save the money to buy the house.

Of course there are many "experts" who are in fact active promoters of debt because they are wanting to sell houses, cars, time shares, small business plans, airplanes, boats, automobiles, credit card accounts, department store accounts, and all kinds of other things. To these persons, debt is something to be encouraged because it brings profit to them or to the company or organization for which they work.

Debt is of course a major problem in North America with credit card debt and mortgages people can't afford causing enormous harm. Many people have huge problems with debt because of unexpected medical expenses that were not covered by insurance.

> ***Debt is not always as bad as some doomsday advisors claim and is also not always as good as some aggressive salespeople claim. The reality is that debt has a place in the lives of most people in North America, but most also need to be far more careful about how much debt they carry.***

Mortgage Debt

You may want to look again at the discussion on home purchases found under *Myth Three* on pages 43–46. As shared at various points in this book, there can be problems with mortgage debt. Mortgage debt becomes problematic when people buy more home than they can afford; when people have an adjustable rate mortgage that increases payments beyond what they can afford; and when the value of a home decreases until it is less than the amount owed on the home.

But most of the time, for most people, a mortgage is the only realistic way to purchase a house or condominium. Even if the value of the house or condominium doesn't increase as fast as it has in prior years, it still remains a sound investment for most people. What is important is being realistic about the price of the house one purchases and getting the best possible deal on a mortgage.

Several so-called "wealth builder" authorities have advocated various real estate strategies in addition to the purchase of one's own home. For example, several have suggested buying a modest-priced house that needs fixing-up; improving its appearance and value heavily through "sweat equity" (purchasing materials but doing almost all of the work personally); and then selling the house at a profit. This is still a strategy that can work if you have the time and the skills to do this kind of home improvement—and if you purchase the house at a good price.

If you don't have the skills, you may be able to develop them learning how to make improvements to your primary residence; and you may also be all right if you have a close friend who is willing to help you learn. I'm very impressed with how skilled some of my friends have become at home improvement through talking with others, asking advice at hardware and home improvement stores, and studying books and Internet information.

There is another, riskier wealth-building strategy that is frequently suggested, especially in late night television info-mercials. That is the strategy of acquiring houses, duplexes, and/or apartment buildings and renting the space to others. Certainly in the tight credit market that exists as this book goes to press, the numbers of people who choose or need to rent rather than buy may be increasing. That would seem to strengthen the value of this wealth-building strategy. But there are some important reasons why this strategy can be risky:

- Most people who pursue this strategy are dependent on the income from renters to make the mortgage payments on the property. But what happens if a renter loses his or her job and can no longer pay rent at the rate you have been charging? Do you evict them from the property? In many parts of the country, evicting someone is a slow and expensive process. Do you lower the rate to something that can be afforded by a person on unemployment compensation? Do you absorb the cost while the person looks for other employment? This can be a very difficult situation, especially for a Christian property owner who feels compassion with the person in financial distress.

- Most people who rent properties, sooner or later, get a renter who abuses the property and generates new expenses for the owner. The expense of repair can readily exceed any security deposit that was made. While the renter is technically obligated to cover the expenses, collecting those expenses can necessitate hiring a lawyer and may still be impossible if the renter has no significant assets that can be attached.

- Renting property also requires quick availability when repairs are needed. If the hot water heater stops working, the furnace needs repair, or there's a leak in the roof, the owner has an obligation to respond quickly.

People who own large numbers of rental properties find the above problems easier to handle. With a large number of rental properties, *most* renters will be meeting payments at any given time and the small number not doing so generally won't destroy the ability of the owner to make mortgage payments. Likewise, the percentage of units needing repair because of renter abuse will not be high enough to be a serious problem. And owners of large numbers of properties generally have a maintenance person on staff who deals with the inevitable repair problems that arise. The same problems, however, can be catastrophic if you only have one or two rental properties, don't have substantial savings, and aren't able to quickly drop other work to do needed repairs.

None of this is intended as an argument against investing in rental properties. It can still be a good wealth-building strategy, but it's important to recognize the issues that can arise in advance—and to have some savings available to help when things don't go as expected.

Automobile Loans

Automobile purchases are discussed some under *Myth Three*, on pages 41–43. Many people need to borrow money in order to have reliable transportation, and there's no need to feel guilt for that. Keep in mind, however, that:

- A used car, if inspected by a reliable mechanic, may be a far better deal than a new car because the rate of depreciation will be so much lower.

- If you have one especially nice car, you may be able to get by with a second car that is considerably less expensive.

- ***People who live in metropolitan areas with excellent public transportation options may find that they do not need an automobile or need just one vehicle rather than two. Trains, buses, taxis, and the occasional rental of a car for a weekend or a vacation may meet transportation needs at far lower cost than vehicle ownership.***

- ***Some metropolitan areas now offer services that let you share the use of automobiles with others. An organization called Zipcars is the major example of this of which I'm aware. People who participate are in a sense the co-owners of automobiles that they use when needed. It's less expensive and more convenient than traditional car rental, and sharing automobiles in this way also makes a contribution to a cleaner environment by lowering the number of vehicles on the road.***

- Check for the best finance rates when you borrow money for a car. If you are purchasing a new car, you may get the best rate through the automobile maker's finance company, but that isn't always the case. Many credit unions give good rates on automobile loans.

- Automobile leases can be good for people who use a car almost exclusively for business, but they are often not so good for people using the car primarily for personal and family purposes. When the lease comes to an end, you have no equity at all in the automobile. You generally have an option to purchase the leased car at a price that was established at the start of the lease if you wish to do so.

Sometimes it's possible to negotiate a better purchase price option when you are making the initial lease agreement. I've been leasing cars for years, and I sometimes haggle before signing the lease agreement over the purchase price at the end of the lease. Since I use the leased car exclusively for business travel, I generally turn it in and lease a new one—but I want the option of a good deal if I decide to purchase it when the lease is over. Dealerships and leasing companies often will negotiate on that. I once bought a car at the end of a lease because my guaranteed purchase price was less than the car was worth at that time. I bought it and then resold it to a friend who knew it had been well maintained. My friend and I split the savings over his having purchased a similar model at retail.

- When deciding on the term for a car loan, be cautious about extending it too long for a low monthly payment. There are two problems with that: First, the longer the term of the loan, the more interest you pay. Second, if you drive the car a lot of miles each year, you may find yourself wanting to trade it before it's paid for. While dealers and financial institutions will often let a person with good credit trade a car that isn't paid for and roll the balance still due into the new loan, that's an expensive way to trade cars. Pay back the loan at as fast a pace as you reasonably can. It's always great to pay the loan off and feel that you can comfortably keep the car for two, three, four, or even five more years. In those years without a car payment, you may be able to save the money to pay cash the next time!

- Parents have a tendency to help their teenage sons and daughters purchase cars of their own, and some parents feel a need to give cars to their children. This reflects considerable generosity, and there are things that young people can learn from the responsibility of having a car of their own, but this needs to be a very thoughtful decision. Even if your son or daughter participates in the cost of purchasing and maintaining his or her own car, the net cost to the household will inevitably be more than if the driving-age child is permitted to responsibly use the family car(s). And helping a son or daughter acquire a very upscale car can set a level of expectation from life that may not be realistic. Certainly, having a car for a teenage son or daughter can be a convenience for the entire household, but there are also things we learn from having to schedule and share transportation with others in the family. I'm not arguing against providing or permitting a car for a teenage driver, but it does need to be a very thoughtful decision. And you need to be clear about the fact that it will almost certainly be an expensive decision!

Credit Cards

So much has been said about the problems with credit card debt by so many different people in books, newspapers, magazines, television programs, radio programs, and the Internet, that I'm not sure how much it's fruitful to say here. Most people reading this book have an awareness of the problems with credit cards, but that doesn't keep many of us from nevertheless making bad decisions about this form of credit.

Properly used, however, there are many good things about credit cards. For example:

- If you pay your credit card statement in full and on time each month, you in essence have the use of the credit card company's money for a period of time each month.

- Credit cards keep us from having to carry excessive amounts of cash.

- Credit card statements give a concise overview of where money has gone and can make it easier to track your spending.

- If traveling out of the United States, credit cards can simplify dealing with expenses in the currency of another country. Check in advance, however, to see what your credit card company charges for processing charges in another currency.

- Some credit cards offer benefits like airline mileage credits for expenditures made on the card, and some even offer you cash back. But if you are paying any interest at all on the credit card, those benefits are coming at a high price.

- The line of credit on a card can be a source of help in the event of a financial emergency such as a major home repair, automobile repair, or medical expense. Keep in mind, however, that the cost of the credit if you have to repay the money over several months or even a few years may be significant. It's always better to have a savings account for financial emergencies. But credit cards can be a help to people at such times who have inadequate savings.

Okay, we've looked at some of the benefits of credit cards, which are significant. Now let's look at an overview of some of the problems with them. You've heard or read most of this before, but most of us need the reminders:

- On credit cards, you are generally paying 18% or even more interest. That's far more than you pay on a home mortgage, a new car loan, or a signature loan from a bank or a credit union. It's the most expensive money that most of us ever borrow.

- Having credit cards tempts us to purchase things that we can't really afford. When we pay cash, we are far more conservative on expenditures. Except in an emergency, the smart way to use a credit card is to pay the balance in full each month—and to not make any expenditure on the card that you can't pay in full at the end of the month.

- Because credit cards are still relatively easy to obtain, it's very easy to end up with a large number of credit cards with considerable debt on each card. Department stores and chain stores frequently tempt people to open charge accounts with the store or chain rather than using Visa, MasterCard, Discover, or a similar broadly accepted card. The department store or chain wants to save the fee that they pay the other credit card companies for the transactions you make (and those fees can run from 1% to 4% of the amount charged). And the department store or chain would be happy to have your interest income rather than see it going to another credit card provider. But the more credit cards you have, the more difficult it becomes to keep track of expenditures.

- Having too many credit cards and too much outstanding balance on those cards can negatively impact your credit rating, resulting in it being more difficult to get a favorable rate on a home mortgage or even having an impact on getting insurance at a good rate.

- And then there is the painful reality that credit card companies are simply out to make as much money from you as they can.

> ***The people who run these companies are not your friends—they want to take as much of your money as they can. They'll entice you with a low introductory interest rate and put in fine print all the things that will end that rate.***

You can have a perfect payment record for years, miss a single payment because you are exceptionally busy, and have them cut off your credit until your account is brought current. You can get hit with high fees for late payments and for going over your credit limit. They may abruptly lower your credit limit and not bother to tell you for days or weeks.

- Financial advisors routinely talk about the importance of shopping for the credit card that gives you the best rate and the best benefits (like cash back or airline mileage credits). It's certainly good to do that. The terms and benefits, however, are rarely static. Credit card companies are notorious for special offers to get your business and then for changing the terms in ways that are not beneficial to you. Don't too quickly drop one credit card for another that promises more benefits. The improved benefits may not last, and the fact that you drop one and add one can have some impact on your credit report. You do have the option, if unhappy with your terms, to call the credit card company and ask for a change. Sometimes they'll do it! Try that strategy before too quickly changing cards on the basis of an initial promise.

In the previous chapter, I wrote about the danger of putting too much trust in salespeople, stockbrokers, financial planners, insurance agents, bankers, real estate agents, and other professionals. What I said in that chapter is an understatement in terms of trusting credit card companies. Don't trust credit card companies at all. They are never your friends. Use the services for convenience and occasional benefit, but never let your guard down!

Using Debt to Improve Your Future Income

It's rarely a good thing to use debt to finance something that is going to go down in value. That's the problem with borrowing money to purchase a car—the car starts depreciating from day one. While you may need to borrow money to have a satisfactory car to drive, you don't want to use debt to finance other things that go down in value with the passage of time. Don't use debt to purchase a boat, a golf club membership, a vacation, or Christmas gifts! You are far better off to wait until you can pay cash for such things. While you may well decide to pay for them initially with a credit card (especially things like vacations and Christmas gifts), you want to the funds available to pay the bill in full when it arrives.

There are potential uses of debt to improve your future income. Under the section on mortgage debt, we looked at a couple of the ways that people use borrowing for real estate to open the potential for increased income in the future. There are a couple of other important ways in which people sometimes use debt to improve options for the future.

The first and probably the most common is the use of debt to pay for higher education, which might include a trade school, a college or university education, or a graduate degree. The costs of education beyond high school are very high. Scholarships, grants, summer jobs, and part-time jobs can certainly help. Some parents have adequate financial means and the willingness to pay for higher education for their children.

But many people are caught in the situation that they can only complete the educational work in a reasonable period of time by borrowing money. The reality is that people who gain a trade school, college, university, or graduate degree have lifetime earnings, on average, that are far higher than those who do not. According to the U.S. Census Bureau, high school graduates earned an average of $31,286 in 2007, while those with a bachelor's degree earned an average of $57,181, a difference of roughly $26,000. While the nature and conditions of these opportunities change, there is a variety of government and even educational institution loan programs that provide preferred interest rates and sometimes even the deferment of interest until after completion of the degree or other educational program.

Don't underestimate the financial burden for the future when you borrow substantial amounts of money to pay for an education. I have a good friend and colleague who is forty years old and only now about to finish paying for the expenses of her undergraduate degree, which she completed in her twenties. The reality for many people, however, is that such education is only possible in a timely fashion through borrowing money. My friend's income is almost certainly two or three times what it would be if she had not completed the college degree.

You can minimize the amount of money that you or your children have to borrow for educational purposes in several ways:

- Be sure to apply for as many scholarship and grants as you can. There are scholarships that go unclaimed each year. Seek help from financial aid officers at the school you wish to attend, seek help from high school guidance counselors who may be familiar with local scholarships, seek suggestions from friends, and do research at the library and over the Internet. The College Board, www.collegeboard.com, Federal Money Retriever, www.fedmoney.org, which provides information on government grants and loans, and www.collegescholarships.org, are a few to start with.

- The high school years are a good time to earn money at summer and part-time jobs and to save that to help on college expenses. Don't let part-time work keep you from getting a good education and having good grades, but do be alert to opportunities to earn and save.

- Large numbers of trade school, college, and university students work in the summer and have part-time jobs during the school year. That helps finance at least some of their living expenses as they pursue their education.

- Keep costs in mind in choosing a trade school, college, or university. Determining the relative value of a degree from various institutions goes beyond the scope of what can be done in this book. It can be true that a degree from an especially well-known and respected institution like Harvard, Yale, Princeton, Notre Dame, or Stanford may give the opportunity to develop relationships and open access to especially high-paying positions. But many people choose to attend small, private, expensive schools from which the degree will not have any more value than a degree from a far less expensive institution. State colleges and universities offer some exceptional values in the quality of education offered at a far lower cost than a private school.

> ***In the part of the country where I live and work, a degree from a major state university like Indiana University, Purdue University, the University of Illinois, the University of Michigan, The Ohio State University, or the University of Wisconsin will likely put you at or near the top of your field and at a far lower price than the private alternatives.***

I anticipate that some readers with strong feelings about alma maters that are expensive have a set of reasons why the cost is justified. That may be right. My major point here is that the cost of the education needs to be weighed against the benefit. There's a private college not far from where I am typing these words that costs more than twice the cost of any state university and whose graduates earn less on average than those with state university degrees. *U.S. News and World Report* has an annual report on values in higher education. That shouldn't be the only criterion for choosing an institution, but it should be one of the criteria.

The second is the use of debt to finance a business enterprise. According to the Small Business Administration, more than

600,000 new businesses are started in the United States each year. Many of these are begun by entrepreneurs who use a combination of personal savings, investment by others, and financial institution loans to start the business. The failure rate for new businesses is high with perhaps as many as thirty percent of new enterprises failing within the first two years. That percentage rises to fifty after five years.

Failure rates, however, do not take into consideration two factors. First, some of these businesses don't continue as they are but are acquired by someone else and given a new name or merged with another business—the fact that they are no longer in business can throw them into the "failure" category but the owner may have come out okay financially. Second, there are many new businesses that do succeed, that create new jobs, and that help stimulate the economy.

My father was an entrepreneur who ran a restaurant, a movie theater, and a tavern. Living in a small town, he had no local competition with the movie theater or the tavern (there was only one liquor license for the area at that time). The restaurant, however, had lots of competition—over a thirty-year period of time, my father averaged a competitor a year. All of them went out of business. When I was a child, I would experience great anxiety when another new restaurant opened up, especially because there always seemed to be a big flow of people to the new place. I thought we would be in financial trouble, and I was distressed that we had so many friends who would try the new restaurant. My father, however, was never worried. He would calmly tell me that it was natural to want to try a new place and that I shouldn't resent people doing that. He would also tell me that running a restaurant well was a tremendous amount of work and that it was very hard to be consistent in quality of food and service.

People would always return to my father's restaurant, and the new restaurant would in time go out of business. The truth is that running a restaurant or any other business is an enormous amount of work and also requires a great deal of knowledge. People generally fail for a combination of these reasons:

- The new business is under-capitalized. There aren't enough funds to provide the quality of facilities, equipment, and staffing needed for success. There aren't enough funds to cover the ups and downs of income over the first several months of business.

- People start the new business without adequate knowledge of what is involved. A person who is excellent at repairing automobiles stops working for someone else and opens a shop of his or her own without understanding issues of scheduling, taxes, other government requirements, cash flow, inventory control, and other factors. A person who is an excellent cook opens a restaurant without adequate knowledge or experience managing others, keeping inventory fresh and adequate, conforming to health department regulations, handling payroll and taxes, and more. A person who wants to be independent pays a lot of money for a franchise of a national company without having the necessary business or marketing knowledge or experience to succeed.

- Changing trends cause many businesses to fail. A number of privately owned video stores have been pushed out of business through more people downloading movies in their homes and ordering from companies like Netflix. The business concept was good, and the stores were well run, but the change in the larger society created an impossible barrier to overcome. The big video chains like Blockbuster have been hit hard by the same dynamics.

- People sometimes fail because they simply underestimate the enormous amount of work involved and find themselves unwilling to work that hard for an income that doesn't seem adequate.

So am I trying to talk you out of any consideration of starting a business of your own? No, that's not my goal. I simply think it is important for people considering the start of a new business to be very much aware of the risks that are involved and to have as many things going for them as possible from the beginning. New businesses can fail; they can also bring tremendous benefits for the people who own them, for their employees, and for our society. There are things you can do to help increase the probability of success and to protect yourself and others in the event of failure. Space doesn't permit an exhaustive treatment here, but a few comments may help you:

Recognize that running a business of your own isn't for everyone. There's nothing wrong with working for someone else! That's what most people do. Don't move to start your own business without thinking carefully about all the skills and background you'll need to be successful.

- You want to have as much cash in hand as possible when you start a new business. The less you have to borrow, the more likely you are to be successful. Banks and other lenders are very reluctant to make loans to new business ventures, and you'll have to present a solid business plan and show that you are investing funds of your own to have any chance of such a loan. I would urge you to resist the temptation to borrow against the equity in your home through a second mortgage or to rely on credit card financing. While those strategies sometimes work, the risk to your financial well-being is very high. You don't want to lose your home if your business doesn't succeed. And the high interest rates for borrowing against credit cards can become another barrier to success.

- Many people start business ventures with financial help from family and friends. You'll find a number of people who give counsel who say to never do this because you are risking the financial well-being of people to whom you are close. I'm not going to go so far as to say that you should never do this. But you should never accept a loan or investment from friends or family if the people providing the funds would be in serious financial trouble if they did not get the money back. Be very open about the risks involved, and be fair in the interest you offer to pay or the percentage of the business you offer for a particular amount of investment. You also need legal advice before accepting money from others. There are laws that affect the circumstances under which one can accept investment income.

- If you do not have a good understanding of the financial aspects of running a business including the handling of payroll and taxes, then gain that knowledge before you begin. You can hire people to help with bookkeeping, but nothing replaces having personal knowledge of the finances of the business. If you have no interest at all in learning these things, then find a business partner who has the needed skill.

- Talk to a large number of people who can give you perspective and counsel. Many communities have organizations of retired business executives who offer free consulting to people starting a new business; that kind of help can be of immense value. Talk to other people who have successfully started new businesses, talk to people who run similar businesses, talk to bankers, talk to real estate professionals if you are needing a building or office space, talk to college or university faculty in business and marketing departments.

- Consider the possibility of taking some college or university courses that would increase your knowledge of running a business. If you are going to do this, however, be sure that you select a school that offers plenty of courses on small business and on entrepreneurial work. Some marketing and business departments are so focused on large corporations that the strategies offered aren't always helpful to a person starting a new business.

- Develop a careful business plan, in writing, before you start. Ask people you respect to read the plan and give you feedback. Identify the potential that exists and the obstacles you need to overcome. As a part of this, develop not just an income and expense budget but also a cash flow budget that projects cash in and cash out for the first three years of operation. A business can sometimes be profitable in terms of income being greater than expense but still not succeed because payments don't come as quickly as expected and funds have to be invested in new equipment or inventory. This business plan will help you make good decisions, and it's crucial to have such a plan as a part of any approach to lenders or investors.

- Pray for God's guidance throughout the process. Ask God to bring you in contact with people who can help you succeed, and ask God to put you in contact with people who will tell you clearly if your chances of success are not great.

What If You Are Already in Crippling Debt?

A few people are reading these words and thinking: "All this advice is fine, but I am already in horrible financial difficulty and don't see how I can get out of the hole that I'm in. I've begun to wonder if filing bankruptcy is something that a Christian should ever consider. I'd like to pay all my obligations, but I'm not sure that's even possible now."

You are not alone if you are feeling in that financial situation. The combination of credit card debt, mortgages with high payments, and lost hours of wages or even lost jobs has placed many people in a precarious financial situation. Medical expenses can be another major factor pushing people into financial catastrophe. Ministers, Christian financial planners, and others are not of one mind on this issue. Here are the two common schools of thought:

- Some, especially in more conservative and evangelical theological circles, feel that a debt is an obligation and that a Christian should never consider bankruptcy unless truly forced into it by creditors. Some take a very hard line on this, saying that even people with overwhelming medical expenses are probably over the edge because they had too much credit card debt before hitting the medical problems. These persons are fond of citing Psalms 37:21 about the wicked borrowing and not repaying.

- Others say that the reality is that people can get into situations that are impossible and need a new beginning, a fresh start. The Gospels, after all, have a great deal to say about grace and forgiveness! And some maintain that the legal tradition of bankruptcy actually is rooted in Deuteronomy 15:1–11 which provides for debt forgiveness every seven years.

Being responsible about money is of course an important part of having a good life, and the Scriptures certainly teach us to honor our obligations. Bankruptcy is an extreme solution to financial problems and should only be used by persons for whom other strategies are not realistic. Excessive debt causes enormous problems for individuals, for families, and for our society as a whole. We need to work hard to avoid excessive debt, and we should never take on debt that we do not intend to fully repay.

Having said that, I feel enormous compassion for people who are living with financial problems that appear to be almost impossible to resolve. While bad decisions have been at the root of many of these problems, the truth usually is that factors beyond the control of people have also contributed to these difficult situations.

The practice of financial institutions packaging home mortgages and selling them to investors meant that those financial institutions had no real stake in whether or not people could repay the loans, especially when adjustable rate mortgages pushed up payment levels so significantly. Likewise, credit card companies have offered people excessive amounts of credit and then have often increased interest rates precisely when people were already in financial difficulty.

The fact that so many people do not have good health insurance has had a devastating impact on many individuals and families. As I write these words, the House of Representatives and the Senate are working on health care reform; but it is too early to know what the impact of that will be. It is certainly true, however, that health care expenses not covered by insurance have put some individuals in a financial hole from which it is impossible for them to climb.

There are people with overwhelming debt who then find themselves in the position of having their pay reduced or even of losing their jobs. Persons in that situation often have no real hope of making all the payments on debt that they were barely able to handle at their previous income level. There are millions of people who have put enormous energy into finding new employment but who have simply been unable to do so.

There are also people who end up deeply in debt to the Internal Revenue Service for unpaid or improperly computed taxes. This is a specialized area of debt that won't necessarily be removed by the same strategies as other debt. If your financial problems are heavily based in large indebtedness to the Internal Revenue Service, then you need legal counsel. The Internal Revenue Service, in spite of its vicious reputation, isn't closed to the possibility of settling your tax bill for a reduced amount if that is truly all you can pay; but you need the counsel of an attorney to work out a fair settlement. Do not attempt to do that on your own.

When I read the New Testament, I hear words of forgiveness and grace far more often than I hear words of judgment and condemnation. I believe that God forgives us for bad financial decisions just as readily as God forgives us for bad decisions in other areas of life. While bankruptcy is an extreme solution, it is the only way to a new beginning for some people. If you are in that category, then you should explore this option. Whether you end up deciding to file for bankruptcy or not, it's very important to adopt new habits in the handling of money that will help prevent you from being in such a situation again.

The regulations on bankruptcy went through some change shortly before the publication of this book, and they are almost certain to go through further change in the months and years ahead. I want to offer just a few simple guidelines that may be of help if you are living with debt so great that it appears you cannot get out of it.

- Remember that bankruptcy is an extreme step and will affect your creditworthiness for a long period of time. Don't go this route unless there are no realistic alternatives.

- Be very cautious about credit counseling services that are offered over the Internet, on television, and in other ways. Many of these are outright scams that will charge you money pretending that they can get your debts significantly reduced when in fact virtually nothing is done for you. Others are services run by subsidiaries or affiliates of credit card companies and financial institutions whose objective is to keep you from filing a bankruptcy and to wrench from you as much interest income as you can possibly pay. They may restructure your debt, but it is not likely to be in a way that is truly beneficial to you. Always check with organizations like your local Better Business Bureau or United Way to find out the reputation of such services. Some communities do have true nonprofit credit counseling services that have no connection with the financial industry and will really seek to help you—but there are relatively few of these services.

- You can sometimes gain ground by talking to officers at lending institutions and credit card agencies. These people do not want you to file bankruptcy, and they are sometimes willing to be flexible on terms to help you avoid that. While the harassment of collection phone calls can make you want to avoid any contact with these organizations, talking with them can be exactly what you need to do. Your best direction in conversation is to take the initiative in calling them and to ask to speak with a supervisor. The people who are calling because you are behind on a payment do not have the authority to change your interest rate or your payment terms, but there are people above them in the structure who do have that authority.

- When determining priorities for payments in tight financial times, remember that you want to keep food, heat, water, electricity, and at least minimal phone service as top priorities.

  Then you want to make rent or mortgage payments and automobile loan payments. While credit card companies can be very aggressive in their telephone and mail collection efforts, the canceling of a credit card doesn't begin to pose the problems of being evicted from an apartment, having the bank foreclose on your home, or having your automobile towed away. Base your decisions on a rational assessment of the money you owe rather than on an emotional response to the pressure of those seeking to collect.

- You may have so much debt that bankruptcy is the only true alternative, and you may need the fresh start that a bankruptcy can give. While it is an extreme move and does have consequences for future credit, a bankruptcy is not going to destroy your life and can make possible a new beginning—in which you can put to work new habits that will improve your financial well-being. While the laws continue to change, you will likely be able to keep your primary house (assuming that you can handle the payments if you aren't also carrying so much additional debt) and some of your pension benefits. You need the help of an attorney in the process including guidance on whether you should file a Chapter 7 or a Chapter 13 bankruptcy. A Chapter 7 wipes out most of your debts and gives you a new beginning. A Chapter 13 is often called a reorganization bankruptcy and lets you pay off debts, at perhaps a reduced level, over a period of time. It's possible that new bankruptcy legislation could change the nature of both Chapter 7 and Chapter 13, so remember that legal counsel is crucial.

- Whatever path you take, including bankruptcy, remember that God continues to love and care about you. God does not hold against you any bad decisions that you may have made in the past, and God does want you to have a new beginning.

It's easy for any of us to become judgmental about the financial situation of others or of ourselves. We may be very hard on ourselves for the unwise decisions we've made and for the mistakes that we've repeated. We may be angry at people we consider irresponsible for having accumulated debts they can't repay. We may feel judgmental toward wealthy people who seem to have taken advantage of others and to be less than generous in their own charitable giving.

The Gospel remains an account of forgiveness, grace, and new beginnings. We are urged to look realistically at our own lives and to let God help us transform our lives. We are also cautioned about being judgmental toward other people. God forgives us and expects us to forgive others and ourselves. The Gospel offers good news to all of us, no matter what our financial situation.

Myth Number Seven

Money problems are the primary cause of marriage and relationship problems.

Like most myths, there is an element of truth in this statement; but it's far too great a generalization to say that money problems are the primary cause of marriage and relationship problems. It's often the case, in fact, that poor communication in marriages and other relationships is what causes the money problems. Couples and families need to learn how to communicate in healthy ways—about money and about everything else.

A teenager in a congregation I pastored told me about an interesting late-night conversation between her parents she had overheard. The high school marching band to which she belonged had an opportunity to play at Disney World. The band members were thrilled, but the trip there from downstate Illinois was going to be an expensive one. Had there been more notice, the band members might have undertaken a major fund-raising project; but because of time constraints, the students were all being asked to come up with their own funding for the plane trip, the hotel, meals, and miscellaneous expenses. That figure came to $850 a person. Her parents were solidly middle class, but they had had some unusually high medical expenses for her brother a few months earlier.

She had slipped downstairs to get a school book she had left in the family room and overheard her parents in the kitchen. This is how she remembered the conversation:

Her mother: "Kelly is really excited about the band trip to Disney World. I wonder if you and I should try to fly down there too so we could see her perform. She hasn't asked us to do that, but I think it's because she knows money is tight. The parents of some of her friends are going down. It would mean a lot to her if we did. I think Matt [Kelly's brother] could stay with his friend Brandon's family while we were gone."

Her father: "I don't see how we can do it. I've actually been regretting the fact that we've just acted like there was no problem with Kelly going herself. But we still owe the hospital over thirty thousand dollars, and we'll have Kelly in college in another two years. I can't see us spending the money to fly down there ourselves."

"Thirty thousand dollars? I had no idea we owed that much money. I know you told me that the insurance wasn't covering everything, but I thought you were talking about a few thousand. Why didn't you tell me it was so much?"

"I should have, but I didn't want to worry you. I felt like I was worrying enough for both of us, and you were already feeling so much stress from Matt's illness. The good news is that he's all right now. That's what counts. We can eventually repay the money."

"But I could have been helping by watching spending. I've just been going along like normal. I wish you'd told me. And Kelly and Matt should know too."

"But think how guilty Matt would feel. He already feels like his illness has taken all the energy of the family. If he knew how much debt we had, he'd feel even worse."

"But we let Kelly think her going was just fine, and we probably shouldn't have done that. It's too late now."

"We'll charge the ticket on our Master Card. I think we can handle the hotel and meals out of our bank account. I wouldn't want her to not go."

"It's hard to say what the right thing is here. I agree that we should still let her go, and I agree that we shouldn't spend the money for us to go. But you and I should have been talking about this. We need a plan for paying the money to the hospital."

"And I don't want us to stop living and make repaying the debt the only thing that we do. The band trip is a big deal for Kelly, and I don't want her to feel guilty about it."

"But we aren't helping her learn about money or about life by not telling her there's a problem. She's going to be away at college in two years and making most of her own financial decisions. We aren't exactly helping her be prepared for that."

Kelly wasn't angry with her parents about the conversation or about their not having told her about the financial problems. Her mother did talk with her about the problem the next day, not knowing that Kelly had overheard their conversation. Her mother explained that they had decided Matt, who was nine years old, was a little too young to be given the load of knowing how high the medical bills were. Her mother made it clear that they wanted her to go but felt badly that they didn't feel they should try to go along to see her marching there.

Kelly was glad that they had finally decided to let her know about the problem. When she talked to me, she was bothered that they had been so slow to talk with her and also that her father hadn't told her mother about the financial problems. She felt that, as a fifteen-year-old daughter, she had a right to know there were problems. She also thought her father had been unfair to her mother, though she recognized that he was trying to protect her.

She made the decision herself to use three hundred dollars of her own savings to help with the expenses of the trip, and she picked up another hundred dollars in baby-sitting money before the trip happened. She felt good about that contribution to the trip and to the expenses of the family.

Communicating about Money

The mother, the father, Kelly, and Matt are all good people who loved one another deeply and also were deeply committed to God and to the church. But they provide a good example of some of the communication problems that happen in families and that especially happen between couples. What can we learn from this?

First, couples need to communicate openly and honestly about financial matters. Kelly's father saw himself as protecting his wife by not telling her about much hospital debt they had, but she wanted to know. She also had a right to know since the debt affected her as well. Because she didn't know, she made different decisions about spending money and hadn't been able to be part of solving the problem. Further, Kelly's father had to carry the whole load by himself, which had to be uncomfortable.

Second, as they grow older, children need to be informed about the status of family finances. While it may have been appropriate to not share the burden with a nine-year-old who had been very ill, the situation reflects how important it is for families to talk about financial issues. Kelly wanted to have the information and was pleased that she could help with the costs of her trip.

Children learn how to communicate about money and about the rest of life in large part through the example of their parents.

Knowing how their parents make financial decisions can play an important role in their making good decisions themselves.

Third, the failure to communicate clearly can make problems worse. Kelly's mother could have made many decisions that made their financial situation worse than it was because she hadn't known the extent of the medical debt.

Fourth, couples should view financial concerns, like the rest of life, as spiritual concerns. These are concerns about which it's appropriate to pray and to seek God's guidance. Making a decision about telling or not telling Matt and Kelly about the medical debt presents a huge parenting challenge. The act of praying about such concerns can strengthen a relationship and strengthen faith.

What's Really Important?

Ross and Bethany had been together for twelve years when Ross became sexually involved with a colleague at his place of business. Ross had a reasonably good job in sales. His wife was an attorney who had an excellent position with a large law firm. She was on the way to making partner, and she generally worked sixty to seventy hours a week. They had two children, and were fortunate that their combined income made it possible to hire a nanny to be with them at the end of the day until Ross got home. Ross took the kids to school on his way to work and was usually the one who prepared supper in the evening.

Bethany had often struggled with guilt over the demands of her career. They had gotten married while she was in law school, and Ross had provided all of their financial support in that period of time. They had their first child while she was still in law school and their second in her fourth year with the large law firm.

Bethany had been very thankful for how supportive Ross had always been of her career and of his willingness to carry much of the load of caring for the children and the household.

When Bethany learned of his sexual involvement with the colleague, she was devastated. He was horribly sorry about the relationship, ended it immediately, and requested a transfer to a division where he would not be seeing the woman on a daily basis. When Bethany and Ross moved past the shouting and crying, they began to realize some of the things that had changed:

- The amount of time Bethany was gone had steadily increased. She had at one time been working fifty hours most weeks and occasionally sixty. But as the carrot of firm partnership grew closer, she began working more like seventy hours most weeks. That made a difference in the amount of their time together.

- They had for years enjoyed a leisurely Saturday morning, sleeping in with each other, making a late breakfast for themselves and the kids, and talking together over coffee after breakfast. They had not done that for almost three years.

- Bethany saw herself as owing a debt to Ross for helping put her through law school and for being so supportive with the kids. She felt that she had an obligation to be successful in the firm in large part because Ross had sacrificed for her to have the opportunity. When she worked long hours, she felt as though she was doing it for both of them. She had been setting aside bonus money so that they could purchase a house on a lake as a weekend get-away.

- Ross never thought of Bethany as owing a debt to him. He also did not have the same interest Bethany had in a vacation home. Given the ages of their kids and the pace of Bethany's work, he thought it unlikely that they would actually spend time in that house even if they could afford it.

- Because of how hard Bethany worked and because of how hard Ross worked between his job and his responsibilities in the home, they were both tired almost all the time. They had sex far less frequently, and they talked far less frequently.

- While it was no excuse for an extramarital relationship, Ross acknowledged that he was lonely for the kind of intimacy that he and Bethany had enjoyed in the first part of their marriage. And the more they talked, the more Bethany realized that she herself felt a similar loneliness.

The desire for professional and financial success certainly played a part in the problems of Bethany and Ross. Some would say that their marriage problems were caused by a combination of too much ambition and an inadequate sexual relationship. The reality, of course, is more complex. Many factors were involved in the loneliness that they both began to experience in the marriage relationship.

This is not a book about marriage improvement! But I want to offer a few additional thoughts about communication in intimate relationships, especially as it relates to money. This continues the list started earlier in the chapter.

Fifth, couples need to have a shared vision of what is important to them in life and of the goals they want to

accomplish. Some of the vision and the goals will no doubt be related to matters of money, but the most important goals for most couples are not financial ones. Common goals for couples who articulate them often include things like caring for each other, raising healthy children (for those who choose to have children), building a strong relationship with each other, developing a close relationship with God, and being people who make a positive difference in the world.

Healthy financial goals help provide the container or the vessel in which other goals can be met. The fulfillment of the financial goals alone will generally not create a strong marriage or bring happiness, but they provide the foundation for other goals to be achieved.

Sixth, couples should not take for granted that they continue to share the same vision and goals. Couples need to be intentional, perhaps at the time of their anniversary each year, about being sure they are still seeking the same major goals. Bethany thought that her success in the law firm was as important a goal to Ross as it was to herself, but that was actually not the case. Neither of them had talked candidly about the price they were paying for her focus on becoming a partner.

If they had talked more openly about the partnership goal, they might have determined together that it was not as important. Or if they had decided jointly that it was an important goal, then the sacrifices to achieve it could have been easier for the two of them to share together.

They did talk about the partnership goal and the lake house goal but within the context of the extramarital relationship. They tearfully determined that their relationship with each other and the care of their children were the most important things in their lives. They decided to drop the lake house as a goal, with Bethany reluctantly acknowledging Ross's observation that it would be difficult to enjoy it as the children grew older and wanted to be around their friends on the weekends. They also determined that, while partnership in the law firm was desirable, there were limits on how much should be sacrificed for that goal. They determined that Saturday and Sunday mornings always belonged to the family and church, not to the law firm. If Bethany couldn't make partner with that change in schedule, then it wasn't worth being partner.

Seventh, couples need time to visit with each other on an ongoing basis. The kind of Saturday morning ritual that Bethany and Ross once had can make a significant contribution to a healthy marriage. Good communication takes time. While it can be pleasant to snuggle together and fall asleep after an exhausting day for both persons, those are not moments for high quality conversation.

It's a very unoriginal idea, but many couples find it beneficial to have a "date night" together once a week or at least a couple of times a month—a time when they are together without children or other adults. It can be dinner out; a picnic (when the weather is good—no picnics in the winter where I live!); a long walk in a park; a visit to a museum; or any other activity that is mutually enjoyed and provides opportunity to talk.

Eighth, couples should not avoid talking about things that are potentially difficult. It's easy to simply avoid unpleasant topics out of fear of how the other person will respond or out of concern to not hurt or worry the other person. Kelly's father kept the full knowledge of their financial problems to himself because he did not want to concern his wife, but that proved no favor to her.

The list of things that married couples and others in committed relationships avoid talking about can be a long one: concerns about children, concerns about money, unhappiness with where they are living, problems at work, concerns about the church, worries about their financial future, and so the list can be continued. Making a habit of being open about such concerns will always strengthen a relationship even if the initial conversations are difficult.

Myth Number Eight

Ministers shouldn't talk to the congregation about money.

Many lay people and many clergy have accepted this myth. Some clergy, in fact, would prefer not to talk about money at all. In one Christian Community survey of clergy, we found that 91% of them reported they were somewhat to extremely uncomfortable talking with the congregation about money. Many pastors fear being criticized if they spend too much time in sermons or in worship service announcements talking about money or about the financial needs of the church.

The reality, however, is that clergy are generally the persons in the congregation who have received the best education about the relationship between money and the spiritual life. Thus clergy have an important role to play in both educational and promotional efforts.

The pastor has the major leadership role in the church. If he or she doesn't clearly communicate that giving is important, many members will conclude that it isn't. The financial program of the church should not be conducted in a vacuum from which the pastor is removed. For the most part, people only respond negatively to the pastor's involvement in financial matters when the pastor himself or herself is overly apologetic or when the pastor exhibits such a preoccupation with finances that it appears money really is more important than people. Most pastors are in no danger of conveying that impression.

The regular teaching and preaching ministry of the minister should provide help to the congregation in areas like these:

- How we deal with living in a consumer-driven culture.

- How we avoid measuring our own worth and the worth of others on the basis of financial accomplishments.

- How we responsibly handle the material resources God has given us—not only what we give to the church but how we handle all that we have received.

- How we can reduce the tremendous anxiety about money that afflicts so many people today.

- How we deal with the kind of power money exerts over us and over others.

- How we can live with a continuing spirit of thanksgiving and an awareness of the countless blessings God has given us.

- How we can better understand the Genesis view of creation and our responsibility for the environment in which God has placed us.

- How we can better understand the needs of the poor and the call of Christ to care about "the least of these."

Choosing the Wrong Car Dealer

I wrote in an earlier chapter about having a very good relationship with a professional car salesman and routinely leasing or purchasing my cars from him or from his son. I've not always been that fortunate! Early in my ministry, I was associate pastor at a fourteen hundred-member congregation. The senior pastor, Walter Theobald, was in many ways like a father in the ministry to me. In the fall of my first year with the congregation, I was ready to trade cars. Carl, a member of the church, was a car dealer, and his agency is the first one I visited to get a price on the car. I did not deal with Carl directly, but I made sure that the salesperson knew the owner belonged to the congregation I pastored.

As I started checking with other agencies, I found that the price I had been given at his dealership was very high. I was pricing exactly the same model and equipment at each dealership. I talked once more to the salesperson at Carl's dealership. He lowered the price slightly, but it remained higher than any other price I had obtained. I bought the car from another agency.

The Sunday after I purchased the car, Carl was in church. On his way out, he shook hands with Walter and myself and then stepped back a couple of paces and said, "Walter, you need to get control of this young man. Buying a car from another agency isn't likely to have a positive impact on the offering plate. I am very unhappy." And he walked out.

I was upset and thought I had made a mistake that would have disastrous financial consequences for the church. Since Carl owned a car agency, I assumed that he was one of the largest givers to the congregation. In fact I had mistakenly thought that he had enough money that he wouldn't care all that much where the young associate pastor bought a car.

When Walter and I visited the next day, he suggested to me that we should find out how much Carl gave to the church before getting too upset about his comment on giving. Fortunately for my mental health, in that congregation, the pastors had access to the giving history of members. We did not often consult that information and always treated it as highly confidential as did the treasurer and the financial secretary. When we checked the giving record, we found that both Walter and I gave more money to the church than Carl. As a matter of fact, a lot of people gave more money to the church than Carl!

Walter did suggest to me a different way that I could have handled the situation that might have produced a different result. He suggested that I should have asked for Carl the first time I went to the agency rather than working with the salesperson. Carl might have turned me over to a salesperson, but my first approach should have been to him. When I discovered that the price from Carl's agency was too high, there was another opportunity to have talked with Carl directly. Walter explained that I could have shown Carl the other prices, explained that I wanted to do business with him, and offered him the opportunity to make a major adjustment in the price.

There was no way to know for certain how much influence Carl had on the price I had been offered on the deal; it may have been the calculation of the salesperson and the sales manager. Walter explained that being a pastor at the church did not put me under an obligation to pay an outrageous amount of money for a car deal.

When I was ready to purchase a second car for my wife, I called Carl and made an appointment to deal directly with him. His initial price to me was hundreds of dollars lower than the next best price that I was offered.

Financial transactions involving people who belong to the congregation can be difficult. There are some people in business who will routinely give the pastor a better deal than anyone else receives. There are also some who will feel the pastor has no choice and will overcharge, sometimes by as much as their annual pledge to the church! Fortunately, through the years, I've gotten more great deals than poor deals from people who belonged to my congregation. What I in fact want is simply a fair deal.

I share the story of my experience with Carl because it illustrates some important points relative to the pastor's role in economic matters:

- It's unrealistic to think that the pastor will not be involved in some financial transactions with members of the congregation. The best guideline is generally for the pastor to approach these transactions as he or she would want to be approached if in the position of the church member. The pastor is not under any obligation to pay an unfair price to a church member, but it's usually a pleasant experience to do business with a member.

- There are other kinds of financial transactions between pastors and members of the congregation. Most pastors will also have to deal with persons in the congregation going through tight economic times who come to the pastor seeking food from the church's food pantry or direct economic assistance. Not all churches have a food pantry; some cooperate with other community agencies to help provide that service. Most congregations have a social action emergency fund, a pastoral discretionary fund, or funds set aside in a similar way to help persons in need. The pastor is generally the person who administers the fund. Being gracious to persons in need and protecting their confidentiality are obviously very important in such relationships. The pastor also has a responsibility to be certain that the funds set aside for that purpose are wisely used.

- There is a direct relationship between stewardship and the spiritual life. Because of that and because of issues like the one that arose with Carl, there are good reasons for clergy to have access to the giving records of the congregation. Walter and I learned that we had less at risk in dealing with Carl than we would have thought otherwise. We also learned something else important: there was something wrong in Carl's spiritual life that was causing him not to be generous with the church. Obviously the teaching and preaching ministry of the church had fallen short in the area of stewardship.

- The incident with Carl caused Walter to reassess what the congregation was doing in stewardship education and what he and I were doing in sermons that related to overall stewardship education. We made some important changes.

The Pastor and Stewardship

A minister friend of mine named Ralph used to believe that it was important for the minister to have no part in the church's annual financial campaign and to have no knowledge of the individual giving of members. He took pride in never attending meetings of the Finance Commission or of the task force assigned the responsibility for the annual campaign.

One year the person asked to chair the annual campaign task force was a man who chaired a couple of nonprofit boards in the community and was considered to be good at raising money. Under his leadership and with no knowledge of the plan on the part of Ralph, the task force designed a plan that was focused on people giving "a fair share." The task force took the amount of money needed for the budget, divided it by the number of households in the congregation, and announced that everyone should aim for that goal with their giving. It was understood that some would do a little less and some would do a little more.

The church budget for that year was $240,000, and there were eighty giving units or households, meaning that $3,000 a year was determined to be the fair share. This approach actually did motivate some people who gave below that level to increase their giving. There were some people in the congregation on very low incomes, however, who could not give that much and who experienced significant guilt as a result. The most serious consequence of this approach was that several people who had been giving significantly more than $3,000 a year determined that they no longer needed to do so and reduced their giving. The financial campaign came up short by almost $30,000.

Ralph's lack of involvement in planning for the campaign combined with the campaign chair's lack of experience doing fund-raising in a church context resulted in some serious mistakes:

- The campaign focused on the "fair share" terminology rather than on a biblical or spiritual theme. The campaign almost completely failed to connect financial giving with the spiritual life with the exception of one sermon that Ralph preached in that period of time. That had a negative impact on motivation and made it feel like a secular rather than a religious campaign.

- There was almost no emphasis on giving in proportion to the manner in which God has blessed us, which is a core concept of all approaches to Christian stewardship. There was a matter-of-fact statement that some would have to give a little less and some a little more than the "fair share," but this only served to make some feel guilty for not having more from which to give and to make some feel they could give less than in the past.

- There was almost nothing in the campaign that helped people think about the extent to which God had blessed their lives. They were not helped to focus on all the good things in their lives.

- The focus of the campaign was far too much on "meeting the budget" rather than on giving in response to God's generosity.

I've written more substantially other places on various approaches to the annual financial campaign of congregations, and Christian Community offers a complete guide to financial campaigns including four different approaches. My purpose in this book on personal finance isn't to tell you how an annual campaign should be run.

What is significant here is that the myth that the pastor shouldn't be involved in financial matters in the church is one that can have very destructive consequences. It can result in a campaign like this one in Ralph's church, which has negative results both for church finances and, more importantly, for the spiritual lives of people in the congregation. At a minimum, the pastor of the church (or one of the pastors in a multiple-staff setting) needs to:

- Work with the Finance or Stewardship Commission or Committee to develop a year-round approach to stewardship education for the congregation. That approach might well include a congregation-wide study of a book like this one that deals with personal financial matters from a Christian perspective.

- As a part of that year-round stewardship education, integrate financial concerns into sermons in healthy ways, speaking to some of the issues identified earlier in this chapter.

- Use the time of the offertory in the worship service as an opportunity for stewardship education, to help people connect their material gifts to the spiritual life.

- Be part of the planning for the annual stewardship campaign or emphasis in the congregation. An annual emphasis is needed in most congregations, even if people have a well-developed connection between their giving and the spiritual life. The annual emphasis provides an opportunity for people to think about their giving to the congregation and for church leaders to know how much income to realistically anticipate so that the church budget is developed in a responsible manner.

- Show by his or her involvement that the annual stewardship campaign or emphasis is an important part of the life of the church. There should be no embarrassment or awkwardness about this.

- Help in the interpretation of special offerings that are taken during the year. Each of those provides an opportunity to connect giving and the spiritual life.

- Be sensitive to financial issues during routine pastoral work in the congregation. If the pastor is not uncomfortable talking about money, people in the congregation are much more likely to be comfortable. There are times when people want to talk about how the church is doing financially and about financial issues in their own lives. During difficult economic times, it's especially important for the pastor to be open to talking with people about the economic trials they are experiencing. The goal of these conversations is not gaining money for the church—the goal is to help people with their spiritual lives.

Myth Number Nine

A tithe (10%) is the correct level of giving for all Christians.

The tithe is a good biblical guideline for our returning to God a portion of what we have been given, and it is the right amount for many middle-class Christians. The larger concept, however, is the realization that everything we have comes to us from God's love. Does God expect 10% from people living in poverty? And is God satisfied with 10% from people of great wealth? The tithe is a good guideline, but it doesn't go far enough in helping us weigh our blessings and life situations.

Walter Theobald, the senior pastor to whom I referred in the last chapter, shared these words about what Jesus is seeking from us:

Jesus isn't seeking a partial commitment of your life.
Jesus doesn't want to claim a certain percentage
of your time
or your abilities
or your money.
Jesus wants the whole thing.
Jesus wants everything you do
to reflect His will and to show His love.

We need to reflect our faith in the way we use our time, in the way we use the abilities that God has given us, and in the overall way we use our money. It's not just a matter of giving 10% to the church; it's how we use everything that God has given us.

Being committed to Christ means that everything becomes a spiritual matter, including how we interact with difficult people, how we make our decisions, how we form our attitudes toward others, and how we share the good news with other people. Christ is after a total commitment from us. When we make that commitment, we open ourselves to the many blessings that Christ wants to give us:

And God is able to provide you
with every blessing in abundance,
so that by always having enough of everything,
you may share abundantly in every good work.
2 Corinthians 9:8 [*NRSV*]

The Blessing of Generosity

A few years ago, at a lunch break at a workshop I was conducting, a woman in her early seventies shared with me her experience with a young man in his late twenties who attended her congregation. Here's how she told the story: "This young man always gets to worship late, and he always comes and sits at the other end of *my* pew. I heard some people say that he did some kind of work with computers and was really smart, but he always looked like a disorganized mess to me. He almost always came to church looking like he'd just gotten out of bed. His hair would be a mess, he was usually unshaven, and his clothes always looked like he'd slept in them. Sometimes I felt like God kept sending him to my pew to annoy me, to punish me for something I'd done wrong.

"Well, on this particular Sunday, he came into church just as the pastor was finishing the morning announcements. There were other people in the pew that week, so he actually ended up sitting right beside me. As he sat down, the minister was describing the horrible plight of a woman about my age in the congregation. Her husband had a long battle with cancer, and they had wanted to try some treatments that weren't approved by their insurance company or by Medicare. They'd borrowed a great deal of money by taking out a new mortgage on their home. When he died and she lost his pension, she didn't have enough money to keep up the payments.

"She was trying to sell the house, but she was so far behind on payments there was a danger of it being foreclosed before it could be sold. The pastor said we were going to take up a special offering right after the announcements to try to raise enough money for her to bring the payments current and keep them up until the house was sold.

"Out of the corner of my eye, I saw the young man take out his checkbook. Well, I was somehow surprised by that. I thought of him as a person who wouldn't even have a bank account. Then I just figured that he would make a gift of ten or twenty dollars, maybe twenty-five. I'm not very proud of this, but I was seated right beside him. So when he made the entry in his check register, I couldn't help myself, I peeked.

"And I was amazed. He had written the check for $825.00, and the register showed that he would only have about $35.00 in his account after he'd written the check. I was just amazed. I supposed that he might have some savings or something, but I'd never bring my own account balance down to just $35.00. His generosity was incredible, and I knew in an instant that I had been completely wrong about this young man."

We think of the word generosity as one that describes a person who readily shares money or other financial resources, like the young man just described. Certainly that is one of the most important meanings of the word in English and of the Greek word that is most commonly translated as "generosity."

Generosity, however, refers not only to the act of giving but to the attitude or spirit with which the giving is done, and the full meaning of the word deals with more than money. If we want to fully understand the fruit of the spirit called generosity, we need to begin by thinking about what God has already done in our lives. Generosity is called a fruit of the spirit because it is a response to our building a closer relationship with God and living with a greater awareness of the blessings of God in our lives.

A friend of mine travels to Haiti each summer to direct a Vacation Bible School program that my home congregation helps fund. I've appreciated her reflections on the relatively harsh living conditions there and on how thankful those conditions have made her for three things: a drink of cold water, a comfortable bed for rest, and indoor plumbing! She has wisely noted that people who live daily with suffering may come to be thankful for things that the rest of us take for granted. She wrote in an e-mail: "When I come home to the States and find my house being maintained at a comfortable temperature and gas in my car and electricity at the flip of a switch, I'll be in a much happier frame of mind than those who've been taking such things for granted."

Many people reading this book who have endured major surgeries or serious illness in their own lives or in the lives of those they love know that those experiences cause a renewed thankfulness for these marvelous bodies we have been given and for the gift of good health. There are many times when we take our bodies and our normally good health for granted. When we do that, we are failing to cherish one of the most marvelous of our blessings from God.

And there are other kinds of blessings. The day before I wrote this chapter was a very productive one. I wrote a major grant proposal to a foundation; I worked my way through three of the four stacks of paperwork that had accumulated in my office; and I responded to something like thirty e-mails. But what I cherished most about the day went beyond the work I accomplished. I had a short but very enjoyable conversation with a couple who asked if I would perform the wedding service for their grandson; I had a pleasant e-mail exchange with a friend from my church about how to handle a PowerPoint presentation in a worship service; I learned that my friend and work colleague Kristen Leverton Helbert, her husband Chad, and their daughter Tess were going to be in town over the weekend; I made plans for a business trip with my friend and colleague Melissa; and I spent a pleasant evening at home with my wife Sara eating pizza and watching a DVD. Those relationships are all part of the blessings of God in my life.

The reality is that we are continually surrounded by blessings from God, even in the midst of very difficult times. But we tend not to stay aware of those blessings. When we take seriously building a closer relationship with God and spend more time in prayer and reflection, we develop a much deeper sense of the blessings that are all around us, and we begin to recognize the presence of God in those blessings.

And generosity then becomes the natural response to our awareness of those blessings—blessings that certainly include the material but that at their deepest involve our relationships with one another and with God. Generosity isn't just the act of giving but the attitude of thankfulness with which we give. There are three kinds of generosity of the heart that should flow as part of the fruit of the spirit.

First, certainly there is generosity of the heart that results in the sharing of our material resources. God has provided us with the blessings that make it possible for us to share. When we recognize the material blessings in our lives, we want to share them. We want to share them with the work of God through the church, with other organizations that are doing work consistent with the faith, and sometimes directly with persons in need.

Now we do live in a time when many organizations are competing for our charitable dollars. My wife and I together attended five institutions of higher education, and they would all like to have as much of our money as they can get. My wife gives to both Bluffton College and The Ohio State University. I managed to successfully stay lost from the University of Illinois alumni office for twenty years, but they were relentless and found me. If there's someone from your past you want to find, don't spend money on a private detective agency—just tell an alumni officer that person is a source of benevolent support and let the alumni office track the person down.

We have to make choices. I make a small annual gift to Garrett Theological Seminary, a graduate school that provided me with an excellent education; but I choose not to give to the universities I attended. Both of those institutions are already well endowed, and they have alumni far wealthier than I! I do my major higher education giving to a seminary I never attended; Bethany Theological Seminary is the only seminary of my denomination, the Church of the Brethren. My support makes more of a difference there; and if we don't have a seminary, then, in my opinion, we cease to be a distinct denomination. That's not an argument against giving to the other institutions; I'm simply sharing the logic of my own giving decisions. Your logic may be different. All of us have to make choices.

Our giving to the congregation should be seen as a different category than our other giving. While no church is perfect, the gathered community of faith is part of the body of Christ; and we have a shared ministry as part of this body. Our giving should flow not out of obligation but out of generous hearts, out of thankfulness for what happens in the church and through the outreach of the church.

What that means in terms of the amount of the gift depends on our individual circumstances. I have a very dear friend who lives on a disability income of $565 a month. She receives food stamps and has subsidized housing, but I truly do not understand how she is able to live on such a limited income. Does it mean the same thing for her to give 10% of her income to the church as it does for someone earning $100,000 a year to give 10% to the church? No, it doesn't. A person who earns $100,000 a year can give $10,000 a year to the church and not be making any sacrifice of well-being. For my friend to give 10% of her $6,780 income to the church would mean her going without food or a warm house part of the time. She barely survives on that income. Does God expect the same percentage from her as from a person with a higher income? I don't think so.

Then what about the person who earns $250,000 a year? Is 10% an adequate level of giving for that person? When I read the enormous number of Christian books on personal finance in preparation for writing this book, I was surprised to find that virtually all the authors feel that 10% is the appropriate standard for a person regardless of how high the income level. But if everything we have is a gift from God, then we have a responsibility to be good managers or stewards of all that income. Living in a world with so many enormous needs, it's difficult for me to believe that 10% is an adequate level of giving for those of us blessed with especially high incomes.

I think about a friend of mine who earns $275,000 a year and also receives an annual bonus that can run as high as $100,000. He determined several years ago that he should be giving at least 25% of his income to the church and other charitable causes. He's increased the percentage through the years and currently gives the church 25% and distributes another 15% to other charitable organizations. He feels wonderful about the good his giving brings about and feels thankful to God for making the generosity possible. He still has a high income, lives in a very nice house, and has adequate savings for the future.

There are people of great wealth who have come to recognize that the best thing they can do with their wealth is seek to make a positive difference in the world. Some of those persons have established charitable foundations that do wonderful things to help those in poverty, to protect the environment, to protect the rights of minorities, to work for peace, to help people relate their faith to important issues, and in other ways to improve the quality of life for others. Some of these persons have given away most of their wealth during their lifetimes, and they feel good about it.

No one can make these decisions for someone else. In the absence of prayerful discernment, however, our spending will always rise at least as rapidly as our incomes. We all need to take time at least once a year to think about the overall blessings we have received and to determine what our giving to the church and to other causes should be. The tithe or 10% is a good guideline for many of us, but it should not be seen as the absolute standard. Remember the larger concept: it all belongs to God!

Second, and this one may surprise you, we should have a generosity of the heart toward ourselves—we should in fact cut ourselves some slack. The woman who talked to me about the young man who had bothered her for so long was truly filled with disappointment in herself for having judged him so harshly. She was far angrier at herself than she had ever been at him. Most of us are our own worst critics. We know, deep down, the failures of our lives, the dark places in our hearts that we hope are never exposed to anyone else, the long list of things about ourselves that we wish we could change. That's true even for those of us who are sometimes accused of arrogance, for the arrogance is generally a mask to cover our insecurity.

The fruit of the spirit, the result of a close relationship with God, is the realization that God loves us as we are, that God forgives us for our failures, that God does not judge us with the harshness with which we judge ourselves.

And third, we should have a generosity of the heart in our attitudes, our words, and our actions toward other people. That was the gift of the spirit which the woman who told me about the young man most wanted to better develop in her own life. Rather than our starting point in relationships being one of judging and evaluating, we should let it be one of warm hospitality and acceptance. Rather than seeing others as potential threats, we should see them as potential blessings, sent to us by God.

We live in a society where people serve their own ends by trying to convince us to be hateful toward or fearful of whole categories of people. There are those who portray illegal immigrants as dangerous; there are those who portray gay, lesbian, bisexual, and transgender people as less than the loved children of God; there are those who seek to convince us that all Muslims are terrorists. We should resist those attitudes, which represent not a generosity of the heart but a betrayal of the heart.

The woman who told me that story had more to say: "After the service, I started a conversation with this young man. He'd introduced himself to me in the past, but I hadn't even remembered his name. I couldn't keep myself from asking if he had known the woman for whom the offering was being taken. He said, 'No, I don't even know what she looks like. But I was so moved by what the pastor said. And I thought about what I've done with my money the last month, about how much of it I've wasted, and I wished I'd done differently. If I hadn't wasted so much, I could have given more to help this wonderful woman who mortgaged the rest of her life to try to gain health for her husband. I hope someday I find someone who loves me that much.'"

Generosity is a fruit of the spirit... a glad and joyful response to the one who loves all of us more than we can ever grasp or imagine.

Myth Number Ten

Estate planning is primarily for wealthy people.

The reality is that everyone needs to plan for what happens near, at, and after the end of life. People need living wills or medical powers of attorney so that others know what measures they want taken if they are in a terminal condition and unable to communicate. Parents need to carefully provide for who will raise their children in the event of their death. Everyone needs to think through what should happen with their assets at the end of life, and most people have far more assets than they realize. And the church should not be forgotten in estate planning.

Beth and David, a wonderful young couple in a church that I pastored, were killed in an automobile accident. They left behind a six-year-old son, Eldridge, and an eight-year-old daughter, Kiana. There were accidental death insurance policies and term life insurance policies on Beth and David, and those policies made possible an estate of about four million dollars. Money to take care of the children was not the issue.

Who would take care of the children was the issue. Both of David's parents were deceased, and Beth's parents were both in poor health. David was an only child, and Beth had one brother who was married and lived a thousand miles away. Edith and Russell, a couple in their mid-fifties who lived next door to David and Beth, had been close friends to them for almost a decade and had embraced Eldridge and Kiana. David and Beth had talked with Edith and Russell about the two of them raising Eldridge and Kiana in the event of a tragedy like the automobile accident. Edith and Russell were very willing to do so.

But nothing was ever put into writing. In the absence of a will or other written instructions, a judge had to make the determination about custody and granted it to Beth's brother and sister-in-law. The relationship between Beth and her brother had not been an especially close one, and the children barely knew him. The fatal accident had happened while Edith and Russell were taking care of the children, and the children had continued to stay in their home until after the court hearing.

At the hearing, Edith and Russell shared with the judge the conversations that they had shared with Dave and Beth and their desire to raise the children. The judge, however, decided to go with the biological bond to the children's uncle and granted custody to him and his wife. Eldridge, Kiana, Edith, and Russell were all devastated by the decision.

The children were staying two more nights in the home of Edith and Russell before being relocated to the home of their aunt and uncle. After the children went tearfully to sleep, Edith and Russell stayed up most of the night talking about the situation. They remembered conversations with Beth about her brother and their strained relationship. Beth's brother had no involvement in a church; he and his wife had two poorly behaved children of their own; and he had a temper that was very intimidating to people around him. Beth had been happy to have little contact with him and would never have wanted him to raise their children.

The next day Russell asked Beth's brother to have lunch with him. Over lunch, Russell outlined a plan. He said that the brother could keep all the money from the estate but that Edith and Russell would like to raise the children. He said they would appreciate it if $200,000 a child could be put into a trust for college expenses for the children but that they wanted nothing for the cost of raising them. They had correctly interpreted the motivation of Beth's brother. When he realized that Edith and Russell were not trying to get the bulk of the insurance money, he was actually relieved to agree to sign over custody to them. His only stipulation was that he thought $100,000 a child should be adequate for college with all the interest it would earn over the years. Russell did not argue.

The children were raised by Edith and Russell, and Dave and Beth would have been pleased by the result. They would not have been so pleased to know that all but $200,000 of the estate ended up in the hands of a brother for whom Beth had no respect. But Edith and Russell had been right about her brother's desire being for the money rather than the children, and they knew what was important to them.

The story had a better ending for Kiana and Eldridge than might have been the case. It was a blessing that Edith and Russell loved the children so much and were willing to do what was necessary to gain custody of them. It might not have worked out so well. And if Edith and Russell had not been comfortably middle class, they might not have felt they could take on the cost of raising two young children at their own stage in life. A will or a trust arrangement could have taken care of everything and resulted in the money being available to Edith and Russell for the cost of raising the children and then the remainder available for the children after they graduated from college.

Technically speaking, as you might suspect, the brother was supposed to be keeping all of the funds in trust for the benefit of the children, taking only what was needed to raise them. But with the move to another state, enforcement of that by the court would have been extremely difficult. Russell and Edith knew that would be the case. The authority of a court is no substitute for wise planning on the part of parents for what happens to custody and finances of children in such a situation.

Wise Financial Planning as a Ministry

Christian Community has published a wonderful book about planned giving called *The Generosity Option* by Tom Rieke, a United Methodist minister and outstanding authority on the topic. Planned giving refers to wills, living trusts, bequests, charitable remainder trusts, life insurance, and other ways of giving that are not strictly based on one's current income. While the booklet is especially designed to encourage people to be generous with the church and other charitable causes, it highlights at a broader level how important it is to make plans for what happens near, at, and after the conclusion of our earthly lives.

We need to think about situations like the one just described with Dave and Beth, about how important it is to provide for the custody and the financial needs of children in the event the parents die while they are young. Wise financial planning for the future has the potential to make a tremendous difference in the lives of people we may never even meet. Consider the account of my friend Harry, which I shared in the introduction to *The Generosity Option*.

"If the government gets all my money when I die, I just don't think I'll be able to enjoy the eternal peace that's supposed to be waiting for me," Harry said and laughed, as he sat across from me in my office. It was early evening. I had been working on a sermon, and Harry had come on the wrong night for a meeting. He'd asked if we could take a few minutes to visit. I was a young pastor, and I wasn't overly comfortable hearing him talk about his own death. Harry's kindness and commitment were so high that it felt to me a shame he couldn't be cloned! But Harry knew death was inevitable, and he had some plans.

"I've got a few specific things I want to do with my estate for my family. But they'll all be fine whether I give them anything or not. The money is mainly a way of reminding them that I care. My granddaughter, God bless her, just wants the old chair that we used to sit in together while I read to her." He smiled and showed me her picture. "What I want to do is make a difference with my money. I'd like to create something that didn't exist before. This community has a lot of teenagers who don't get much help from their parents and who get in trouble with the law. I'd like to see a program created that could change their lives, and I'd like to do it through the church."

The result, a few years after our conversation and a few months after Harry's death, was a substantial gift to the church that enabled it to create a program for teens that reached into the community. Thousands of lives have been changed for the good by Harry's dream and generosity, and the congregation has developed a passion for outreach to youth.

Harry gave me my first exposure to the impact that planned giving could have. Planned giving, at its best, can result in lower taxes and financial benefits for the donor; and it can also result in substantial financial resources for the church or other recipients. But money is not the primary reason for planned giving. Consider what planned giving can make possible:

- It can deepen the spiritual life of the donor, resulting in a closer relationship with God and a healthier view of financial resources.

- It can produce a feeling of satisfaction, of making a difference in the life of the donor.

- It can make a tremendous difference in the life of the church or other charitable recipient, sometimes opening whole new areas of ministry.

- It can change the lives of many people not known to the donor or the church but who are touched by the impact of the gift.

Some of those reading these words may be thinking: "This isn't for me. I have more debts than assets." OR "My estate will be so small when I die that there's no point in my making elaborate plans." OR "This kind of thinking is for people in the later years of life. I have plenty of time before I plan for my death."

Most of us, in fact, have greater financial worth than we realize. Some of us forget about term life insurance policies that may be part of the benefits provided by our employers. In the process of making payments on a house, we may forget that the house itself increases in value almost every year. Many of us have funds in pension programs, IRAs, and other savings plans that we do not think about on a daily basis. If you added up the value of all your assets and subtracted from that the amount of all your liabilities, the figure might surprise you. Whatever the dollars involved, we want to remain faithful to Christ and to those we love—to make a positive difference with what we have been given.

Over the course of my ministry, I've had the privilege of seeing tremendous impact from people who planned carefully for their own future, for the future of those they loved, and for the responsible use of their assets beyond their own lifetimes. As I sit in my study writing these words, I remember not only the young people affected by Harry's generosity but also...

- The inner-city children who were able to experience summer camp and interaction with people of other backgrounds through a scholarship program that was funded by a person's planned giving.

- The senior citizens on limited incomes who received care in an outstanding nursing home because of the planned gifts the facility had received.

- The African-American congregation that received the seed money for a desperately needed building through a foundation created by a man who had never been in their church.

- The three children of parents who died in an automobile accident. Their parents, fortunately, had made plans for their care and for the financing of their education.

- A physician whose practice in a poor South American country was made possible through the support of a charitable foundation funded by the planned giving of many people.

- A church's unique outreach to alcoholics and drug addicts, which was underwritten by the planned gifts of two people whose lives were transformed by that parish.

- A mentally handicapped adult whose future was protected by the careful planning of her loving parents while they were alive.

- A woman who had spent her whole life fighting to get ahead financially and who had begun to feel empty because she felt so poorly connected with people. Her decision to use her wealth for the sake of others opened her heart to new relationships that transformed the last years of her life.

- The young people served by a gymnasium built through the proceeds of a life insurance policy of a young adult who had expected to live for decades but had at a very early age made plans to help others.

- The hundreds of single parents served by a high quality day care center that was the vision of a group of low and middle-income church members. They used planned giving as a means to make their dream become a reality.

All that we have comes to us from the generosity of God. And in that generosity, God has made it possible for us to make a difference in the lives of others. As Paul wrote in his second letter to the church at Corinth: *And God is able to provide you with every blessing in abundance, so that by always having enough of everything, you may share abundantly in every good work* [2 Corinthians 9:8].

Decisions and Documents We Need

1. We need to determine how we want medical decisions made for us in the event that we are unable to make those decisions for ourselves. My friend John, near the age of 80, ate a pleasant breakfast with his wife and went into the living room to his favorite chair to read the morning newspaper as he did on a daily basis. His wife came into the living room a few minutes after and found that John had died sitting in the chair. A stroke or a heart attack had claimed him with no warning.

Of course it was a horrible shock for his wife to find him, but it was a quick and relatively easy death for John. He and his wife were deprived of the opportunity to say the last words they might have wished to each other, but they were spared the agony of a prolonged illness. And John was such a well-organized person that his preferences for the memorial service and a trust fund that held assets jointly with his wife were current.

Death comes in many ways, and it doesn't come as quickly or as easily for many people as it did for John. In the time in which we live, many deaths take place in hospitals or nursing homes following prolonged periods of illness and numerous medical procedures. I think of another good friend of mine whose father suffered from Alzheimer's and remained in a vegetative state for years with no one having the authority to remove the life support that would have permitted a relatively peaceful death. The assets of the family were sucked away maintaining a vegetative state that he would have hated had he been aware of it.

In spite of all the sophisticated and often wonderful medical procedures that are available to us today, the death rate remains steady at 100%. We eventually do die, and our Christian faith teaches us that the best is yet to come as we pass from this life to the next. Most of us have limitations on how many procedures we want to endure to be kept alive if the quality of our lives has markedly deteriorated.

Decisions about withdrawing medical care and permitting death are personal, moral decisions. A full discussion of this goes beyond the scope of this book. What I want to emphasize is that it is important for us to think in advance of what we want to happen if our health has significantly deteriorated and we are not able to make decisions for ourselves. We need to be intentional about those decisions, and we should talk about them with those we love.

My mother was very clear with me and with her primary physician about what she did and did not want done to prolong her life if she could not recover enough to live independently. When she went into the hospital for the final time, I was absolutely certain what procedures were and were not acceptable to her. The physicians and the nurses were fully cooperative with her desires and did all they could to make her comfortable. I was able to stand beside her and hold her hand as she took her final breath.

My mother had been careful to communicate clearly to me and to her primary physician. She also saw to it that I had a Medical Power of Attorney for her and a copy of her living will so it was clear that any decisions I made were consistent with her desires. There are three documents that you should consider having:

A Living Will, which describes what medical procedures you do and do not wish to have done should you become unable to communicate your own wishes.

A Medical Power of Attorney, which gives clear authority to another person to make medical decisions for you if you are unable to make them for yourself.

A General Durable Power of Attorney, which gives authority to another person to manage your personal and financial affairs should you be unable to do so for yourself.

Forms for these are widely available over the Internet and are available through most attorneys for only moderate expense. Some hospitals have living will and medical power of attorney forms available. I almost included such forms in this publication, but legal requirements can vary from one state to another and can change over time. It's better for you to seek the most recent forms yourself. While you may want to have signed copies of such forms in a lockbox at a bank, these are forms that you also want to have readily available. Both you and the person you designate as having power of attorney for you should have copies of the forms.

2. Most people want to communicate in writing what they would like done in terms of their memorial service. For example:

- Do you want a traditional burial, or would you prefer to be cremated?
- Do you have preferences on the kind of casket you want?
- Do you have preferences on where you want to be buried?
- What hymns would you like used for your memorial service?
- Is there a particular pastor you would like to have conduct your memorial service?
- Are there favorite passages of Scripture you would like used for your memorial service?
- Do you want your memorial service held in the church or at a funeral home?

Writing out your desires and sharing them with your family and your church can make the decisions far easier for members of your family at the time of your death. Even if you do not have strong preferences concerning the memorial service and burial, letting others know that in advance will be helpful to them.

Many funeral homes market advanced planning and advanced payment for funeral services. This is a good business practice for them because they receive payment while you are still alive and they are guaranteed your business! This practice is not necessarily such a good one for you and your family. If you select prepayment, take the time to calculate how this really works out financially. While the funeral home may be guaranteeing a price for future services, consider the length of time that they will be in possession of your funds. I have seen very few instances in which people benefited by prepayment. Also consider the possibility that life situations change and that you may find yourself in a different city at the time of your death.

When people make decisions like this while in their forties, fifties, sixties, or even seventies, they often do not anticipate the possibility of a move to another location. I have elderly friends who prepaid for services in Illinois when they were in their early seventies. When their health deteriorated in their early eighties, they moved to California to be close to their son and to enjoy a warmer climate. What had appeared to be a good arrangement for funeral services for them was no longer suitable.

For most people, it's a far better practice to work out these preferences within the family. Clergy have significant experience helping with funeral and memorial service arrangements, and they are a less biased source of advice than funeral home employees. I am not meaning here to be critical of funeral home employees, and I have deep appreciation for the empathy and compassion I've seen demonstrated by many of them over the years. But they are in business to sell services, and they can't help the reality that this impacts the counsel they give. Some churches find it beneficial to offer periodic seminars on planning memorial services.

3. If you have children who are young enough to be dependent on your care and your financial support, then you need to decide to whom that responsibility will be entrusted. The account of what happened to Beth and David makes clear why it is so important to do this.

4. You need to decide how you want the assets of your estate of be distributed when you die. If you have a spouse or a significant other in your life, then you may well want everything to pass to that person. You also need to consider, however, what you would want done with assets should something happen to both of you. In one Christian Community survey of church members, we found that 55% did not have a will, a living trust, or some other legal instrument that would control what happened to their assets at the time of their death.

5. You need to decide what charitable causes you would like supported from your estate. The amount of that charitable support, of course, depends on your stage in life. If you are married with young children, then obviously you want most of your estate going to your surviving spouse and children. If your children are grown and financially independent, then you and your spouse may wish to make some significant charitable gifts from your estate.

6. Your desires concerning items three, four, and five above need to be reflected in a will, a living trust, or other appropriate legal documents. In Chapter Five of this book, I shared cautions concerning the role of many professionals in our lives. But when it comes to being sure your estate wishes are adequately expressed in legal documents, I strongly encourage you to seek the advice of an attorney who has experience in these matters. Unless your estate is very complicated, that advice is not generally expensive. If your estate is complicated, then you need that advice even if it is costly! Not having the advice can be much more expensive.

There are many people for whom a relatively simple will is the best route to take, and you may be able to find the format for a will on the Internet. Even if you do that, I would encourage you to at least have a conversation with an attorney to be certain the format you have selected for the will is one that meets legal requirements in your state. There are other questions that should be considered. In some states, a legal entity called a "living trust" can make things much easier than a will because it avoids your estate having to go through the legal process called probate, which can be time-consuming and expensive. There are other forms of trusts that may also be beneficial to you, your family, and charitable organizations. The counsel of an attorney will help you make the best decisions.

A Concluding Word on Perspective

I had a taxi driver in Washington D.C. who told me that the previous week he had been in a no parking zone to let a person out at a convenient location. The driver went to the trunk of his car to get out his passenger's suitcase and dropped his keys—through a grate in the street into the storm sewer! It was impossible to recover them. By the time he had gotten a ride to his home to get his extra car keys and returned, his taxi had been towed. The process of recovering the taxi took most of the rest of the day, and the towing fee and fine together totaled $500.00. He told me that he felt horrible about how the day had been and felt very sorry for himself.

Then he said that the next morning his first fare was a young soldier, returned from Iraq, who had lost both of his legs. The driver told me, "I looked at this fine young man and what had happened to him, and I realized that car keys down a storm sewer and $500 lost weren't that big a thing at all. It's a matter of perspective. And we sure do need to remember our blessings."

In this chapter and the others in the book, I've sought to give you as much practical advice as possible about financial decisions from a faith perspective. I hope and pray that the book has been useful to you. Financial decisions are important because all that we have comes to us from the grace of God, and our decisions about money can improve the quality of our lives and of the lives of others.

But living is about far more than money, and the blessings that God shares with us are not just financial blessings. The taxi driver was very wise—he recognized that a small financial difficulty was insignificant in comparison to health and other blessings. In the midst of whatever financial problems life brings you, remember that God is always with you and seeking to bless you—in this life and in the life to come.

Now to him who by the power at work within us
is able to accomplish abundantly far more
than all we can ask or imagine,
to him be glory in the church and in Christ Jesus
to all generations, forever and ever. Amen.
Ephesians 3:20–21

Guidelines for Discussion if Studying this Book with a Group

- No one should ever feel on the spot to share something in this group that makes them feel uncomfortable. "I pass" is always an acceptable response.
- It's possible that some persons in the group will feel comfortable enough to share specifics about their own financial situations. When that happens, remember that all of us sharing in the study have a responsibility to hold in confidence things that others share.
- Some of what is shared in this study may challenge some of your preconceptions about spirituality or about personal finance. Work to keep an open mind as you read the book and as you share in group discussion. While you may decide that you do not agree with all the concepts that are presented, the study has the possibility to bring about significant improvements in your spiritual and financial life if you have a spirit of openness.
- This is a study that has significant potential to improve the quality of the financial and the spiritual lives of those who are participating. As part of your prayers during this study, pray for your group together to have positive impact, pray for the person or persons who are leading discussion, and pray for the others who are part of the group.

Study Guide:

Ten Money Myths:

A Guide to Personal Finance

for Christians

Suggestions for Using This Study Guide

1. This study can be used in adult Sunday school classes, spiritual formation groups, Bible study groups, fellowship groups, small groups, church boards, lead teams, mission groups, or staff groups focused on exploring the relationship between spirituality and personal finance. This *Guide* may also be used for individual study, but some suggestions are group-oriented.

2. Some sessions may offer more activities than time permits. Extra suggestions may be carried over to the next session, or you may choose those most suitable for your group's interests, needs, and size.

3. The *Guide* provides sufficient material for 13 sessions but may be used for a smaller number of discussions, depending on your schedule. Choose the combination of topics most beneficial to your group. In some instances, you may want to scan the intervening material and share a short summary of it where needed to maintain continuity.

4. Remember that every group has both active and passive learners. Try to involve participants in a variety of ways, remaining sensitive to personalities and preferences. Encourage, but do not force, participation. Allow "I pass" as an acceptable response.

5. Having class members use different translations of the Bible will enrich your discussions and give new perspective.

6. Discussions will flow better if you read the designated chapter in *Ten Money Myths* and the accompanying session in this Guide before the time of the class or group meeting. There are also some sessions for which you may want to photocopy one or more pages from the book so that group members do not have to

write in their books. The session plans assume that you will photocopy the indicated materials and that a chalkboard, white-board, or newsprint is available each week. You will want to have Bibles available for each participant, or encourage them to bring their Bibles with them. Other needed preparation will be indicated in the session.

7. The fourth session introduces the group members to the possibility of experimenting for a month tracking expenditures and intentionally living as cheaply as possible. Persons who do this exercise generally learn a great deal about their personal finances including how to gain better control over expenditures. This study guide offers an opportunity at the start of the fifth, sixth, seventh, eighth, and ninth sessions for people to talk about their experiences with this experiment in living cheaply. Be careful that people who elect not to be part of the experiment are not caused to feel guilty, but offer as much positive encouragement as you can to people to participate. Our experience is that people who take part in this experiment have a good time in the process.

8. Be sensitive throughout the study to the reality that there will likely be people in your group who are in very tight financial situations. Some of them are in that situation through circumstances over which they have had no control. Some may be in that situation because the myths exposed in this book have trapped them. You want to be careful in presenting the information and in leading the discussions to avoid causing people to feel guilt to the extent that you can. You also want to be very careful that people never feel on the spot to talk about their own financial situations. The first session introduces some guidelines for discussion that are important.

Session One: Introduction

Myths about Money

Overview: Our culture has encouraged the acceptance of several myths about money that contribute to frustration, lowered self-esteem, lowered giving to charitable causes, and sometimes disastrous personal and family financial choices. A healthy understanding of the role of money in our lives and of the relationship between finances and the spiritual life can transform us in powerful ways.

Leader preparation: Put the questions for the first activity on chalkboard, whiteboard, or newsprint. *Optional for the fourth activity: Record a portion of a television newscast that deals with financial concerns and play that for the group. OR bring in a current newspaper and share headlines that relate to financial matters.*

Introduce the group to a few guidelines for the discussions that will take place:

- No one should ever feel on the spot to share something in this group that makes them feel uncomfortable. "I pass" is always an acceptable response.
- It's possible that some persons in the group will feel comfortable enough to share specifics about their own financial situations. When that happens, remember that all of us sharing in the study have a responsibility to hold in confidence things that others share.
- Some of what is shared in this study may challenge some of your preconceptions about spirituality or about personal finance. Work to keep an open mind as you read the book and as you share in group discussion. While you may decide that you do not agree with all the concepts that are presented, the study has the possibility

to bring about significant improvements in your spiritual and financial life if you have a spirit of openness.

- This is a study that has significant potential to improve the quality of the financial and the spiritual lives of those who are participating. As part of your prayers during this study, pray for our time together to have positive impact, pray for the person or persons who are leading discussion, and pray for the others who are part of the group.

1. Invite group members to share in talking about what they learned about money and spirituality from their parents. If your group is larger than seven, consider dividing into groups of three to five persons for the discussion:

- What are the lessons that your parents taught you about money by how they handled their finances and by what they said about money?
- What did your parents teach you about the relationship between God and money?

2. Read or summarize the account of the 33-year-old who was about to lose her home and of the response of the elderly farmer. Discuss: How did this account make you feel? What kind of spiritual witness did the woman make in her frank sharing with the workshop group? What kind of spiritual witness did the farmer make?

3. Pages 14–15 share three valuable perspectives from Scripture. Talk about the three perspectives:

- Matthew 6:25 reassures us that God will see that our needs are met. Why is it difficult for us to accept this reassurance in our contemporary culture? Do you think this reassurance is contingent on some minimal effort on our part? Why, or why not? How does this reassurance relate to the account of the 33-year-old?

- 2 Corinthians 9:6–8 urges us to share out of thanksgiving for what we have and promises us we will have enough to share. Can you identify times when you have given to the church or other causes grudgingly? If so, how does that contrast to the times you have given out of thanksgiving? Do you truly believe that God can be trusted to give us enough to share? Why, or why not? How does this relate to the account of the elderly farmer?

- Exodus 36:5 actually describes a time when people gave more material than was needed for the building of a house of worship. A basic Old Testament theme is that we give to God first rather than giving from our leftovers. Why is it important to give to God first rather than waiting to see what we have left? What blessings come to us when we honor God as the source of all that we have?

4. Money matters are part of our daily lives. Invite group members to share examples of stories in the news in the past week that dealt with money. *Optional: Record a portion of a television newscast that deals with financial concerns and play that for the group. OR bring in a current newspaper and share headlines that relate to financial matters.* Discuss: Why are money matters so often in the news? Do you think our society focuses too much or financial matters or too little on financial matters? Why? What role should the church have in helping us think about personal finances?

5. Talk about the concept of "money myths" as explained in the introduction. You may want to take a look at the Table of

Contents to see the myths that will be discussed in future sessions. Ask: What are some examples of myths that are not related to money? Why can myths exercise great control over us even when we know rationally that they are not true? Why is it important to identify and understand myths about money?

6. Close with prayer.

Session Two: Myth One

Your worth and happiness are determined by what you earn and by what you own.

Overview: In a downward economy, people who internalize this commonly held myth are going to find their self-esteem in the basement and their happiness at the mercy of forces they can't control. A deep faith and healthy understanding of Scripture give people the perspective to find meaning and happiness no matter what the shape of the economy is.

Leader preparation: Obtain one index card and a pen or pencil for each person.

1. Focus on the first four bullets on pages 17–18. Hand each person an index card, and ask them to put the numbers one through four on them. As you read the four questions in the bullets, have people respond by writing *very often, often, sometimes, or rarely.* (For bullets that have more than one question, the one to ask is the first one that starts with "How often. . . .")

Collect the index cards, shuffle them, and redistribute them within the group. Ask the questions again, having class members raise their hands in response to the answers on the index cards they now hold. Talk about each of the questions and the follow-up questions in the second and fourth bullets.

2. Talk about the questions in the fifth bullet on page 18: Do you feel at times as though persons of wealth have considerably greater influence on the events of life than more ordinary people? Do you compare yourself negatively to such persons? Or do you fear that your spouse, children, or parents compare you negatively to such persons?

3. Go around the group, asking those who are willing to answer this question: What are the two material possessions, aside from your home, that are most important to you? Then discuss as a group: In what ways are our material possessions blessings to our lives? In what ways can our material possessions become too important to us?

4. Summarize the account of the author's experience with the young woman at the airport who mistakenly took his computer. Discuss: Why did she feel so uncomfortable at the college she had been attending? Why was she concerned about the possibility that her parents would be disappointed in themselves? Why is it so difficult in our culture to distinguish between our worth and our wealth?

5. Have a volunteer read Ephesians 3:18–21. Then look at the four points on blessings that are shared on pages 23–26. Discuss: How do you feel about the concept that God is always seeking to bring blessings to us? What are some examples of times that God has blessed you but not necessarily in the way you had anticipated? Why is it important not to measure our blessings just in terms of money and material possessions?

6. Close with prayer.

Session Three: Myth Two

God wants you to be wealthy; if you aren't, you are failing to follow God's guidance.

Overview: Many television evangelists and some best-selling Christian authors try to convince us that all who follow God are going to be wealthy. That's not the promise of Scripture. We are promised that we will always have enough to be generous and that God desires to bless us—but not all the blessings are material.

Leader preparation: Obtain one index card and a pen or pencil for each person.

1. Give each person an index card and a pen or pencil. Have people put the numbers one through five on the card and then respond to each of the following questions:

(1) Think about the very first job that you had for which you were paid other than work that you may have done for your parents. Write one of these words to describe how you feel about the compensation you received: *fair (appropriate compensation for the work that you did); underpaid (unfair compensation for the work that you did); generous (more than fair compensation for the work that you did).*

(2) Now think about your current job or if not currently employed the last job that you had. Write one of these words to describe how you feel about the compensation you received: *fair (appropriate compensation for the work that you do); underpaid (unfair compensation for the work that you do); generous (more than fair compensation for the work that you do).*

(3) Have you had a time that you felt like a failure because you have not done better at making and/or managing money? Write *yes* or *no*.

(4) Have you had a time when you felt that you would have done better with your life financially if you had been more faithful to God? Write *yes* or *no*.

(5) As you think about your life as a whole, do you feel that your most important material needs have been met? Write *yes* or *no*.

Collect the index cards, shuffle them, and redistribute them within the group. Ask the questions again, having class members raise their hands in response to the answers on the index cards they now hold. Talk about each of the responses with the group. People may choose to share experiences that they have had related to these questions; don't put anyone on the spot to share, but be aware that several may choose to do so. You may find that this discussion takes most of your group time.

2. Share the author's experience talking with the Pennsylvania factory owner as shared on pages 28–29. Discuss: Why do you think the business owner felt that his financial problems might be because he had failed God? Do you think that fear of this was right or wrong? Why? What does this experience say about our attitudes toward wealth?

3. Have a volunteer read Matthew 11:28–30 in the *Message* translation from page 29. What do you think our Lord means by the "unforced rhythms of grace"? What is the difference between living a life focused on those rhythms and a life focused on acquiring wealth?

4. Pages 29–32 give four guidelines for how we view our work. Summarize those guidelines, and talk about them. Ask: Which guidelines seem most relevant to your life? Which guideline seems to you the most difficult to recognize or follow? What additional guidelines would you offer?

5. Have a volunteer read the Henri J.M. Nouwen quote on page 32 on praying for concrete things. How comfortable do you feel praying for concrete things? Why is it important to pray at times for concrete things? Look at the bullets on pages 33–34 that share the various forms in which God may respond to our prayers; which of these have you experienced in your own life?

6. Close with prayer.

Session Four: Myth Number Three

Having additional money would solve all of your financial problems.

Overview: Many people are trapped into the magical thinking that a windfall of money or increase in income would solve all of their financial problems. While having more money certainly can help for a time, our desires too often increase faster than our finances. Having a healthy financial life depends more on learning to live *within* the income we have.

Leader preparation: Make four copies of page 40 for each member of your class or group. Have two notecards and a pen or pencil for each group member.

1. Ask group members to make a list on the first notecard of the first five things they would do with the money if they inherited or won in a lottery ten million dollars. (You do not need to collect these notecards.) Then summarize the account of the lottery winner on pages 35–36. Have people share, as they feel comfortable, what they listed as the first things they would do with the money.

2. Point out that virtually all of us feel at times that having more money would be a major help with our problems, but that the reality is we have limited ability to control what we earn. The theme of this chapter is that we have a greater ability to control what we *spend*! Invite people to think about the last week, to identify money they spent that was not absolutely essential, and to list the amounts of that money on the second notecard. Have them total the amount.

Collect the index cards, shuffle them, and redistribute them within the group. Have people share the amounts written on the notecards that they are holding (rather than their personal amounts). Write those figures on chalkboard, whiteboard, or newsprint. Ask the group: Are these figures overall lower, higher, or about what you would have expected? Why is it helpful to think about our ability to control expenditures?

3. Summarize the suggestion on pages 37–39 of making "cheap" into a game. Invite people to take part in the one-month experiment suggested by the author. Distribute the extra copies of page 40 that you made so that people will have that format available. Explain that there will be opportunity each of the next four weeks to talk about the experiences people have in saving money and that there will be opportunity for a final discussion of the experience in Session Nine. Make it clear that persons are certainly not required to do this exercise for a month but encourage them to consider participation.

4. Take perhaps ten minutes of time for people to brainstorm their best ideas for saving money. Write those on chalkboard, whiteboard, or newsprint. Point out that the author has provided a substantial list of suggestions, by category, on saving money. Not everyone will agree with every idea in the book or on the brainstormed list. The point is to stimulate our thinking and our action.

5. Have a volunteer read Matthew 6:19–24. What does Jesus mean in saying that we cannot serve both God and money? How can learning how to reduce expenditures help lower our anxiety about money?

6. Close with prayer.

Session Five: Myth Four–A
(Two Sessions on Myth Four)

You can't manage your finances without a budget, and a budget is a great deal of work.

Overview: Most of the popular religious and secular financial management programs that are sold involve complicated forms and record-keeping that look very intimidating to the average person. While those are great approaches for some people, there are several less intense strategies that can help people get a better grip on their personal finances. And a better grip on personal finances helps people be more generous with the church.

Leader preparation: The conversation in the first activity will be helped if you come prepared to share some personal experiences in living "cheaply." Make copies of pages 63–66 for group members.

1. This concludes the first week in which group members have been invited to record expenditures and savings. Invite people to share the experiences they are having. Has it been harder or easier than expected? Has it been enjoyable or difficult? What are people learning about money in this process?

2. Summarize pages 55–57, which talk about the author's experiences with "budgeting" as a child. Invite group members to share their own experiences with money from childhood and experiences they may have had with their own children. Why are these early experiences important? To what extent is it more difficult or less difficult to handle money as adults?

3. Summarize pages 57–60 on "How Much Focus on Money?" Give special attention to the categories in the chart on page 58. Invite group members to share their thoughts and feelings about how much focus in one's life should be on money. Ask: Why is being financially unaware such a danger in our society? Is

being financially aware at all in conflict with trusting in God to provide? Why, or why not?

4. Have a volunteer read Matthew 6:25–34. In the Sermon on the Mount, Jesus seems to advocate a style of living that is almost reckless! Turn the other cheek; forgive enemies; go the extra mile; give to those who beg; don't worry about money. Is there any inconsistency between these words of Jesus and living a financially aware life? In what ways can being financially aware actually serve to lower our anxiety about money?

5. Point out the information on budgeting found on pages 63–74, which includes a form for identifying income and expenses. Distribute copies of pages 63–66. Invite people to spend some time during the week working at compiling this information. Explain that the conversation will be continued in the next session, and give the reassurance that no one will be asked to share their budgeting information with the group. There will be opportunity for people to talk about the *process* of identifying income and expenditures.

6. Close with prayer.

Session Six: Myth Four–B
(Two Sessions on Myth Four)

You can't manage your finances without a budget, and a budget is a great deal of work.

Overview: Most of the popular religious and secular financial management programs that are sold involve complicated forms and record-keeping that look very intimidating to the average person. While those are great approaches for some people, there are several less intense strategies that can help people get a better grip on their personal finances. And a better grip on personal finances helps people be more generous with the church.

Leader preparation: The conversation in the first activity will be helped if you come prepared to share some personal experiences in living "cheaply."

1. This concludes the second week in which group members have been invited to record expenditures and savings. Invite people to share the experiences they are having. Has it been harder or easier than expected? Has it been enjoyable or difficult? What are people learning about money in this process?

2. Invite people in the group to spend some time looking at Genesis 1–3. These three chapters include two different accounts of the creation. As they look at the chapters, ask them to note verses that talk about the responsibility that we have been given for creation. Then talk about those verses. Ask: In what ways is the healthy management of our money a part of being responsible for creation? How do our expenditures relate to the care of the world in which God has placed us?

3. Don't put people on the spot to share their income and expenses from pages 63–66. Do provide opportunity to discuss:

How difficult have those of you who have been working at it found developing a full list of income and expenses? Did anyone have the positive experience of identifying a source of income or assets that had been overlooked? Which expenditures are most easily overlooked?

4. Summarize pages 71–74 on the purpose of budgeting and tracking expenditures. Note especially the experience of Christian Community recorded on page 72 with the fifty households who tracked expenditures all reporting that they spent less. Talk as a group about the different approaches to budgeting and tracking. What are the pluses and minuses of each approach? What seem to group members to be the approaches that are most personally realistic?

5. Close with prayer.

Session Seven: Myth Five

Salespeople, financial planners, stockbrokers, and bankers have your best interests at heart.

Overview: Most of these professionals are good people, and these are professions found in most congregations. The reality, however, is that we are in a consumer-driven culture; and most professionals only make money when their customers spend or invest money. People who want to have healthy financial lives must learn how to avoid being overly influenced by the intended and unintended pressure of others. Too many people have been talked into houses and cars they can't afford and investments that carry too much risk for their life situation.

Leader preparation: The conversation in the first activity will be helped if you come prepared to share some personal experiences in living "cheaply."

You will likely have a salesperson, a stockbroker, a financial planner, or some other professional in your group. The intention of this session isn't to be unfair or unkind to such professionals. The intention is rather to remind people that they are responsible for their own decision-making. It's important to be clear about that so any salespersons or professionals in the group do not feel a need to defend themselves. You'll find that most salespersons and professionals are in agreement about the importance of people taking the final responsibility for their own decisions.

1. This concludes the third week in which group members have been invited to record expenditures and savings. Invite people to share the experiences they are having. Has it been harder or easier than expected? Has it been enjoyable or difficult? What are people learning about money in this process?

2. Summarize the experiences with automobile salespersons shared by the author on pages 75–76. How do you feel about the salesman who talked the author's friend into buying a car when the friend had been resolved not to do so? Was there anything unfair about his tactics? Why, or why not? Why is it our responsibility to make the final decisions about expenditures? Why is it dangerous to let ourselves be too influenced by salespersons and other professionals?

Invite people to share their own experiences of having someone exert too much influence. How did the experience make them feel about the professional? How did the experience make them feel about themselves?

3. Have a volunteer read the story of the wise men and Herod in Matthew 2:1–12. Discuss: What were Herod's motivations in dealing with the wise men? Do you think Herod intended any harm to the wise men? What kept the wise men from doing what Herod wanted? We see Herod pursuing his own goals and wanting to use the wise men to accomplish them. In what ways do the goals of professionals in a consumer society make it easy for them to become users of customers and potential customers? Obviously comparing their activities to Herod isn't quite fair! But just as the wise men had the responsibility to make their own decision about what to do, so do we have that responsibility in commercial transactions. Read aloud the box on page 78 about stockbrokers and financial planners.

4. Summarize what is shared on pages 79–82 on "the less than completely honest." Invite group members to share experiences that they have had. Then look at the box of cautions on page 82. What additional cautions would group members add?

5. The author has written this chapter to warn of the danger of blindly following the advice of salespersons and other professionals, and that is a very needed caution in taking control of our

personal finances. Invite group members to spend some time talking about the positive influence that salespersons and other professionals can be as long as we are careful to be responsible for our own decisions.

6. Close with prayer.

Session Eight: Myth Six

Debt is always good or always bad (depending on the "expert" involved).

Overview: Debt is of course a major problem in North America with credit card debt and too expensive mortgages causing enormous harm. That doesn't mean that debt is always bad as some doomsday advisors claim or that it is always good as some aggressive salespeople suggest. People need a healthy view of the benefits and risks of appropriate borrowing at appropriate times in life.

Leader preparation: The conversation in the first activity will be helped if you come prepared to share some personal experiences in living "cheaply."

This session talks about the impact of debt on our lives. You almost certainly have members of your group who are dealing with too much credit card debt and other financial problems. You may have members of the group who are unemployed. You could have members struggling with decisions about bankruptcy. Be sensitive to these realities during the discussion. Some people who are financially secure and financially aware can be very judgmental toward persons in serious financial trouble. You want this to be a session that offers practical advice and that does so with a spirit of compassion toward any who may be having personal difficulties.

1. This concludes the fourth week in which group members have been invited to record expenditures and savings. Invite people to share the experiences they are having. Has it been harder or easier than expected? Has it been enjoyable or difficult? What are people learning about money in this process? Note that next week will be the final one for discussion about this experience.

2. This myth focuses on financial debt. There are also other kinds of debts in our lives, and there are many that we are unable to repay. Most of us owe a debt to our parents for the love and the care that they gave us. We may owe debts to employers and coworkers for help that they have given us. We may owe a debt to the church for the difference it has made in our lives. And we certainly owe a debt to God. Invite group members to brainstorm the nonfinancial debts that we have, and make a list of those on chalkboard, whiteboard, or newsprint.

3. Now invite group members to brainstorm the problems that people have because they have accumulated too much financial debt. Put those on chalkboard, whiteboard, or newsprint. Ask: In what ways does our culture encourage too much debt? How can heavy debts affect our relationships with other people? How can heavy debts affect our relationships with God?

4. Talk about these kinds of debt and about when they are wise and unwise for a financially aware person. Refer to material in the chapter where appropriate.

- Mortgage debt
- Automobile debt
- Credit card debt
- Debt to improve your future income
  - Educational debt
  - Business debt

    As you discuss business debt, consider inviting people to briefly brainstorm ideas for new, profitable businesses!

5. The last section of the chapter deals with the problems of "crippling debt." Have a volunteer read Deuteronomy 15:1–11 which provides for debt relief every seven years. Then talk about:

- What suggestions of the author for dealing with crippling debt sound the most helpful?

- How do you feel about the Deuteronomy concept of a fresh start for people with crippling debt? How does bankruptcy contribute to that possibility?
- What is the appropriate response of the church to helping people who have crippling debt? If you had crippling financial debt, why would compassion from the church be of importance to you? What are the limitations on what the church can do to help?

6. Close with prayer.

Session Nine: Myth Seven

Money problems are the primary cause of marriage and relationship problems.

Overview: Like most myths, there is an element of truth in this statement; but it's far too great a generalization to say that money problems are the primary cause of marriage and relationship problems. It's often the case, in fact, that poor communication in marriages and other relationships is what causes the money problems. Couples and families need to learn how to communicate in healthy ways—about money and about everything else.

Leader preparation: Note that this is the last week for discussion about the experiment in living cheaply that group members have been invited to experience.

1. This concludes the experiment in living cheaply in which group members have been participating. List on chalkboard, whiteboard, or newsprint the things that people feel they have learned or gained from this experience.

2. Summarize the experiences of the family described on pages 111–115. Discuss: What were the positive motivations of the father in not telling the rest of the family about the high medical bills? What would have been a better way for him to have handled the situation? How do you feel about the decision not to tell their son about the extent of the bills for his care?

3. Look at each of the four guidelines on communicating about money that appear on pages 114–115. Discuss: Which of these guidelines seem to you the most difficult to follow? What do children need to learn about handling money as they are growing up? Why is it important for partners to be open with each other about finances and to share together in financial decisions?

4. Summarize the account of Bethany and Ross that begins on page 115. Then look at the biblical account of David and Bathsheba that can be found in 2 Samuel 11:1–21. Discuss: What are the major factors that caused problems for Bethany and Ross? What are the major factors that caused the situation with David and Bathsheba? What role did finances play in the problems of Bethany and Ross? What role did finances and power play in what happened with David and Bathsheba?

5. Look at the four additional guidelines that appear on pages 117–120. Discuss: Which of these guidelines seem to you the most important? Which are the most difficult to follow?

6. Close with prayer.

Session Ten: Myth Eight

Ministers shouldn't talk to the congregation about money.

Overview: Many lay people and many clergy have accepted this myth. Some clergy, in fact, would prefer not to talk about money at all. The reality, however, is that the handling of money is a spiritual matter; and the minister is the person in the congregation who is generally best qualified to help people understand the spiritual dimension of personal finance.

Leader preparation: If your minister is available, invite him or her to be present to share in the discussion of this session.

1. Invite group members to share their observations about what the church should do to help people relate their spirituality to their financial decisions. List their thoughts on chalkboard, whiteboard, or newsprint. Then invite people to discuss the ways in which a minister can help the congregation in those areas.

2. Summarize the experiences of the author with Carl as those are shared on pages 122–124. Ask: How do you feel about Carl's attitude toward the young minister? What could the young minister have done to avoid the problem that he experienced with Carl? What did he learn from the experience? How should clergy handle financial dealings with people in the congregation?

3. The apostle Paul was not reluctant to talk about money and its role in our spiritual lives. Have volunteers read the following biblical passages:

- 2 Corinthians 8:1–15
- 2 Corinthians 9:6–12
- 2 Corinthians 11:7–11
- Philippians 4:10–20

- 1 Timothy 6:6–10

Ask: Why did Paul feel it was important to talk about the place of money in our lives? Why is it important for clergy to help us in this area? Why do you suppose clergy sometimes feel uncomfortable talking about money?

4. Look at the list on pages 128–130 of things the pastor should do related to spirituality and finances. Ask: Which of these seem to you most important? Which of these seem to you most difficult? What things would you add to this list?

5. Page 122 gives a list of topics with which the teaching and preaching ministry of the church should help people. Ask: Which of these topics can you remember being covered in a class or a sermon? Which of these topics seem to you most important for our time?

6. Close with prayer.

Session Eleven: Myth Nine

A tithe (10%) is the correct level of giving for all Christians.

Overview: The tithe is a good biblical guideline for our returning to God a portion of what we have been given, and it is the right amount for many middle-class Christians. The larger concept, however, is the realization that everything we have comes to us from God's love. Does God expect 10% from people living in poverty? And is God satisfied with 10% from people of great wealth? The tithe is a good guideline, but it doesn't go far enough in helping us weigh our blessings and life situations.

Leader preparation: Have a notecard and a pen or pencil for each group member. Note that the discussion that is part of the first activity with the notecards could end up taking most of your session time.

If possible, obtain some statistics from your church treasurer or financial secretary about giving patterns in the congregation. You obviously don't want to request information about any person's individual giving, but it can be helpful to know how many households or giving units fall into financial ranges like these:

$20,000 or more
$10,000 to 20,000
$7,500 to 9,999
$5,000 to $7,499
$3,000 to 4,999
$2,000 to 2,999
$1,000 to 1,999
$500 to 999
$499 or less

1. Give a notecard and pen or pencil to each group member. Have people number from one to four and then respond to each of the following questions:

(1) Approximately what percentage of your income (after income taxes) do you give to the church? *Discuss after the cards have been shuffled: Are you surprised by the figures here? What would it mean to the church if each of us increased giving by 2%?*

(2) Approximately what percentage of your income (after income taxes) do you give to other charitable causes? *Discuss after the cards have been shuffled: How do you think most people make decisions about the charities other than the church that they support? In what ways do some of these charities also do the work of Christ? Is it possible to give too much support to other charities and not enough to the church? What is different about giving to the church than to other charities?*

(3) In comparison to five years ago, are you giving a larger percentage of your income to the church now, a smaller percentage of income, or the same percentage of income? Write one of these words on the card: *Larger, Smaller,* or *Same*. *Discuss after the cards have been shuffled: What are some of the factors that motivate people to give more? What are some of the factors that cause people to reduce their percentage of giving? How do changed financial circumstances affect the percentage a person can give?*

(4) Would you like to be giving more to the church than you currently are? Write *yes* or *no* on the card. *Discuss after the cards have been shuffled: What are factors that keep us from giving as much to the church as we intend? How would our giving be changed if we truly gave to God first rather than from the leftovers?*

Collect the index cards, shuffle them, and redistribute them within the group. Go through the items, talking about the responses as you go using the questions that follow each item. You may want to write the percentages on chalkboard, whiteboard, or newsprint.

2. If you have them available, look at the statistics for giving in your congregation. Discuss: Are these figures higher or lower than you would expect? If everyone tithed, what would these figures suggest were the income levels of people in the congregation? What do we do as a congregation to help people who join the church think about their level of giving?

3. Summarize the story that the woman at the workshop told the author as shared on pages 132–133. Ask: How do you feel about this level of generosity? What motivated the young man's giving? Try making a list of the various factors that motivate our giving to the church.

4. Look at the three perspectives on generosity of the heart that are shared on pages 135–140. Ask: What does it mean to give out of generous hearts rather than out of obligation? Why should some persons consider giving considerably more than 10%? Why may it be unrealistic for some persons to give as much as 10%? Why does the tithe, or 10%, continue to represent an important guideline for our giving?

5. Close with prayer.

Session Twelve: Myth Ten

Estate planning is primarily for wealthy people.

Overview: The reality is that everyone needs to plan for what happens near, at, and after the end of life. People need living wills or medical powers of attorney so that others know what measures they want taken if they are in a terminal condition and unable to communicate. Parents need to carefully provide for who will raise their children in the event of their death. Everyone needs to think through what should happen with their assets at the end of life, and most people have far more assets than they realize. And the church should not be forgotten in estate planning.

Leader preparation: Have a notecard and a pen or pencil for each group member.

1. Give a notecard and a pen or pencil to each group member. Have them number one through five and then respond to the following questions:

(1) Do you have a will, living trust, or similar estate planning document? Write *yes* or *no*.

(2) Do or did your parents have a will, living trust, or similar estate planning document? Write *yes* or *no*.

(3) Is the church included in your estate planning? Write *yes* or *no*.

(4) Do you have a living will or medical power of attorney to direct decisions in the event you are ill and unable to communicate your own wishes? Write *yes* or *no*.

(5) Do you have written plans for what you would want to have happen in your memorial service or funeral service? Write *yes* or *no*.

Collect the index cards, shuffle them, and redistribute them within the group. Go through the items, talking about the responses as you go.

2. Summarize what happened with David and Beth and their children as shared on pages 141–143 of the book. Discuss: What does this experience say about the importance of planning for the care of young children? What do the actions of Edith and Russell say about their priorities in life?

3. Page 144 begins a section on "Wise Financial Planning as a Ministry." Why is wise financial planning a ministry? How is our view of our assets changed when we truly recognize God as the source of everything?

4. Look through the decisions and documents that are shared on pages 148–154. You may already have discussed some of these items during the first activity. Provide clarification where needed, and encourage group members to follow-up on any decisions or documents that they do not personally have.

5. Have the group read together Ephesians 3:20–21 as found in the book on page 155, and then share in a closing prayer.

Session Thirteen: Wrap-Up Session

This is a final, wrap-up session for those studying the book during a full quarter and having thirteen sessions available. Your group may well have remaining concerns to discuss that can profitably fill this time. Here are some other suggestions for a final session:

- Invite group members to generate a list of things that they have learned through this study. Write those on chalkboard, whiteboard, or newsprint.

- Go through the Ten Myths list again, using the Table of Contents in the book as a guide. Ask group members to identify the most important concept or idea that they gained from looking at each myth. Then invite group members to brainstorm their own list of additional myths about money and faith.

- Have group members look again at the account of creation in Genesis 1–3. Talk together about what it means to take seriously the concept that everything we have comes from God. This study has focused on the financial or material aspects of being a steward of what God has given us. List together what seeing God as the creator of every thing means for our care of the environment and for our relationships with one another.

- Look again at the chart on page 58. Talk about what it means to live a life of financial health.

- Close with prayer.

Resources

Here are publications and resources on spirituality and stewardship from Christian Community, the organization that developed **Ten Money Myths**. All Christian Community resources are based on careful research and practical testing of strategies in congregations from thirty different denominational traditions.

Ten Money Myths: A Guide to Personal Finance for Christians. There are many myths about money that impact our lives as Christians—bringing harm to our financial lives and to our spiritual lives. This book is a frank look at those myths combined with practical advice that balances healthy financial planning with healthy spirituality. This book avoids the trite and often manipulative advice that has so often been associated with Christian financial planning. The book has been written for personal use, family use, or class/group study. $14 each for 1–9 copies; $9 each for 10–30 copies; $7 each for 31 or more copies.

Cell Phones, Dessert, and Faith. Designed for individual, small group, or church-wide study, this book by Steve Clapp provides an easy-to-read, non-threatening way to encourage your members to look at stewardship in ways they might not have before. Topics include: how eating dessert first relates to giving to God first; exploring why we worry about money; debunking the myth that "if I just had a little more money, everything would be all right"; recognizing that everything we have comes from God, including our health, wealth, time, friends, and families. $15 each; $9 each for 10 or more.

Dessert First Devotional Booklet. This booklet provides a 28-day devotional study designed to help readers connect financial giving with their spiritual lives. Devotionals include:

- "Eat the Pie First!" Eating dessert before our meal and giving to God before we give to or pay for anything else.
- "A Perfect Chocolate Soufflé." Understanding that there is a place for good things in the Christian life and that we honor God when we try to do our very best.

$5 each for 1–25, $4.50 each for 26–50, $4 each for 51–75, $3.50 each for 76–99, $3 each for 100+.

Turning Water into Wine: Helping Your Church Meet Financial Challenges. This book is filled with practical counsel to ministers, treasurers, finance or stewardship commissions, church boards, and others concerned with the current state of church finances. The book takes a frank look at the current financial situation in North America and in the world; looks at the relationship between money and faith; offers tested advice on how to deal with tough budget decisions in the church; gives strategies for treating people with kindness in hard times; offers effective strategies for increasing financial giving; and shows how to think outside the box in getting things done in the church. $17 each for 1–9 copies; $10 each for 10 or more copies.

Dessert First Complete Financial Commitment Program. This stewardship package draws on Christian Community's extensive research to provide your congregation with four options for your annual commitment program: Cottage Meetings, Celebration Sunday, Pass It On, and Every Member Visitation. You can choose the most appropriate strategy for your church at this time and use the other options in future years. Each option directly connects congregational giving to the development of the spiritual life and helps participants focus on how giving is directly connected to spiritual health. This complete kit also includes:

- A notebook packed with detailed instructions for all four campaign options.
- A separate packed of materials ready to photocopy (photocopy permission is included).
- A CD with letters in several software formats for customization.
- ***Dessert First Devotional Booklet***; ***Cell Phones, Dessert, and Faith***; and ***Turning Water into Wine***

$165 each including permission to photocopy.

Planned Giving Package. This package includes three resources that will help your church understand planned giving and how to set up the appropriate methods to encourage planned gifts. This package includes one copy each of:

- ***The Generosity Option: Planning Options for Contemporary Disciples*** by Thomas C. Rieke. This booklet covers the questions people often have about planned giving.
- ***Funds for the Future of the Church*** by Thomas C. Rieke, which contains strategies and information which have not previously been this accessible for church leaders. It not only provides the basics but also how to develop a comprehensive planned gifts program.
- ***Forms & Formats for the Local Church***, which contains forms you'll find helpful in setting up current and planned giving programs.

$75 each.